Personal Saving, Consumption, and Tax Policy

Edited by
Marvin H. Kosters

The AEI Press

Publisher for the American Enterprise Institute
WASHINGTON, D.C.

1992

Distributed by arrangement with

UPA, Inc.
4720 Boston Way   3 Henrietta Street
Lanham, Md. 20706   London WC2E 8LU England

Personal Saving, Consumption, and Tax Policy/Marvin H. Kosters, editor
    p.   cm.
    ISBN 0-8447-7015-9—ISBN 0-8447-7013-2 (pbk.)

Printed in the United States of America

Contents

CONTENTS

Contributors

J. GREGORY BALLENTINE is a principal in KPMG Peat Marwick's policy economics group and is the firm's national director of tax analysis. Mr. Ballentine specializes in the analysis of international transfer pricing and other issues in the economics of taxation. He has published widely on the economics of taxation. He participated in the formation of tax and spending policy in his positions as deputy assistant secretary for tax analysis in the Department of the Treasury and as associate director for economic policy at the Office of Management and Budget.

LLOYD BENTSEN is chairman of the Senate Finance Committee as well as vice chairman of the Joint Committee on Taxation. He has served in the U.S. Senate since 1971 and in 1988 was the Democratic nominee for vice president. He served in the House of Representatives from 1947 to 1955. Before his election to the Senate he was president of Lincoln Consolidated and a practicing attorney and judge in Texas.

MICHAEL J. BOSKIN is chairman of the President's Council of Economic Advisers. Previously he was the Wohlford Professor of Economics at Stanford University and the director of the Center for Economic Policy Research. Mr. Boskin is the author of *Too Many Promises: The Uncertain Future of Social Security* and *Reagan and the Economy: Successes, Failures, Unfinished Agenda*, as well as numerous articles in professional journals.

JOHN E. CHAPOTON is a partner at Vinson and Elkins in Washington, D.C. Prior to this, Mr. Chapoton served as tax legislative counsel and then as assistant secretary for tax policy at the Department of the Treasury. He has practiced law in Houston, Texas, specializing in federal tax matters. Mr. Chapoton is a member of the American Bar Association, Section of Taxation, and a member of the Texas State Bar Association.

ROBERT EISNER is the William R. Kenan Professor of Economics at Northwestern University. Professor Eisner's research interests include the determinants of business investment and the development of extended measures of income and output. He has written extensively and testified before various government groups on the issues of monetary and fiscal policy, depreciation, employment, and economic growth. He is the author of several books, including *How Real Is the Federal Deficit?* and *The Total Incomes System of Accounts.*

WILLIAM G. GALE is senior staff economist at the President's Council of Economic Advisers. He is also assistant professor in the department of economics at UCLA. Mr. Gale's research interests include public finance, effects of government credit subsidies, and determinants of saving.

MARVIN H. KOSTERS is a resident scholar and director of economic policy studies at the American Enterprise Institute. He was formerly a senior economist at the President's Council of Economic Advisers and held senior policy positions at the Cost of Living Council and at the White House. His research and writing has been primarily on government regulation policies, labor market issues, and wage trends.

LAURENCE J. KOTLIKOFF is professor of economics at Boston University and research associate at the National Bureau of Economic Research. Previously Mr. Kotlikoff was a senior economist with the President's Council of Economic Advisers. He has served as a consultant to the International Monetary Fund, the World Bank, the Organization for Economic Cooperation and Development, and several U.S. government and international agencies.

WILLIAM A. NISKANEN is chairman of the Cato Institute. Previously he was a member of the President's Council of Economic Advisers, the director of economics at the Ford Motor Company, and assistant director of the Office of Management and Budget. He has also served as a defense analyst for the Pentagon, the Rand Corporation, and the Institute for Defense Analysis. He is the author of *Reaganomics: An Insider's Account of the Policies and the People* and the editor of *Regulation* magazine.

LARRY J. OZANNE is a principal analyst in the tax division of the Congressional Budget Office, working primarily on the topic of IRAs and additionally on analysis of capital gains taxation. Prior to this work he spent several years at the Urban Institute, and he has also served with the President's Commission on Housing and with the Federal Home Loan Bank Board.

RUDOLPH G. PENNER is a senior fellow at the Urban Institute and is former director of the Congressional Budget Office. Some of his earlier posts in government include assistant director for economic policy at the Office of Management and Budget, deputy assistant secretary for economic affairs at the Department of Housing and Urban Development, and senior staff economist at the President's Council of Economic Advisers. He is the editor of *Taxing the Family* and the author of numerous articles on tax and spending policy.

WENDELL E. PRIMUS is chief economist for the Committee on Ways and Means and staff director of the Subcommittee on Human Resources of the U.S. House of Representatives. He is primarily responsible for budget-related analysis and was deeply involved in drafting the Gramm-Rudman law. Previously Mr. Primus was an assistant professor of economics at Georgetown University. His interest in social policy has led to the publication of several articles on health economics and child care.

ROBERT D. REISCHAUER has been the director of the Congressional Budget Office since 1989. In June 1975 he helped set up the CBO and then served as assistant director for human resources and community development and later as deputy director. In 1981 Mr. Reischauer became the senior vice president at the Urban Institute. In 1986 he joined the economic studies program of the Brookings Institution as a senior fellow. Mr. Reischauer has written extensively on federal budget policy, Congress, social welfare issues, poverty, and state and local fiscal problems.

JOHN KARL SCHOLZ is assistant professor in the department of economics and the Robert M. LaFollette Institute of Public Affairs at the University of Wisconsin, Madison. He was recently a senior staff economist at the President's Council of Economic Advisers. Mr. Scholz's research interests include public economics, applied econometrics, and corporate finance. He has written extensively on such topics as savings and IRAs.

CHARLES L. SCHULTZE is a senior fellow at the Brookings Institution and was formerly the director of its economic studies program. Mr.

Schultze has served as chairman of the President's Council of Economic Advisers and director of the U.S. Bureau of the Budget. He has taught at Stanford University and the University of Maryland, and he has written numerous books and articles on a wide range of economic issues.

JONATHAN SKINNER is associate professor in the department of economics at the University of Virginia and research associate at the National Bureau of Economic Research. He has served as a consultant to the World Bank and taught at both the University of Washington and Stanford University. Mr. Skinner's research interests include the economics of housing, taxation, and motivation for personal savings and wealth accumulation.

JOEL B. SLEMROD is professor of economics and of business economics and public policy at the University of Michigan. His prior positions include senior staff economist for tax policy at the President's Council of Economic Advisers and national fellow at the Hoover Institution. Mr. Slemrod has been a consultant to the U.S. Department of the Treasury, the Canadian Department of Finance, and the World Bank. He is currently coordinating the National Bureau of Economic Research project on international taxation, and he is the editor of *Do Taxes Matter?: The Impact of the Tax Reform Act of 1986.*

RICHARD H. THALER is the Henrietta Johnson Louis Professor of Economics at Cornell University's Johnson School of Management. Mr. Thaler is also a research associate at the National Bureau of Economic Research. His research addresses the gap between economics and psychology, stressing the importance of adding behavioral realism to economic models by relaxing the strict rationality assumptions normally imposed.

DAVID A. WISE is John F. Stambaugh Professor of Political Economy at the Kennedy School of Government. He is also area director for health and retirement programs and director of the economics of aging project at the National Bureau of Economic Research. Prior to coming to Harvard, he worked as an economist at the Department of Labor. His recent research has focused on the saving effects of IRAs and other retirement saving programs, labor force participation and the retirement of older workers.

Foreword

Federal taxation of personal income was changed frequently during the 1980s. By the end of the decade, the personal income tax base was broader and most marginal rates were lower than in 1980. Both aggregate revenue and personal saving incentives were affected.

The low personal saving rates of the 1980s, together with public sector dissaving, raised concerns about the sufficiency of savings to finance capital investment and led to proposals for personal saving tax incentives. Other concerns—about income levels and distribution, for example—have led to proposals that would also move away from low marginal tax rates and the neutrality goals emphasized in the tax changes of the 1980s.

Recent tax policy proposals include provisions for restoring and expanding the role of Individual Retirement Accounts (IRAs), for reducing payroll tax rates, for raising personal exemption levels for children, and for converting personal exemptions to refundable credits. These proposals raise questions about the effects on personal saving, the distributional impact of changes, and the effects on tax revenues.

To examine these issues, the American Enterprise Institute sponsored a conference on July 9, 1991, that brought together research scholars, policy analysts, and public officials to assess the effects on saving incentives of the changes in personal income taxation that took place in the 1980s. It also reviewed the research evidence about the influence of IRAs on personal saving, analyzed the effects of other current tax proposals on consumption and saving behavior, and assessed the adequacy of projected savings for financing investment and meeting other future commitments. This volume is based on presentations at that conference, and its publication is intended to make these analyses available to a broader range of scholars, analysts, opinion leaders, and government officials with policy responsibilities.

CHRISTOPHER C. DEMUTH
President, American Enterprise Institute

xiii

1
Introduction

Marvin H. Kosters

The 1980s produced changes in the tax code that were unprecedented in their frequency and in their substantiveness. The reduction in personal income tax rates in 1981 was followed by a series of base-broadening changes that culminated in the more substantial reduction in marginal income tax rates incorporated into the Tax Reform Act of 1986. The changes enacted in 1986 were phased in during the following two years, and other changes were enacted pursuant to the budget agreement of 1990. A number of proposals for still further change were introduced in the 102d Congress in 1991.

Although recent proposals for change contained provisions with a variety of approaches, many included provisions that would affect saving and retirement. Several of the proposals called for broader eligibility for tax-advantaged saving vehicles, such as restoration of traditional Individual Retirement Accounts (IRAs) for most taxpayers or introduction of new varieties of IRAs to encourage personal saving. The sluggish performance of the economy in the last part of 1991 intensified public, congressional, and administration interest in considering tax changes, although this was accompanied by some shift in attention toward proposals that would stimulate consumption instead of encouraging saving. Nevertheless, provisions intended to encourage personal saving were included in the 1992 tax proposals.

Economic Performance and Saving

In discussions of the performance of the U.S. economy, experience during the 1950s and 1960s is often taken as a point of departure with which subsequent experience is compared. Thus, aggregate economic performance in the 1970s was characterized by higher inflation and lower growth in real wages than in the 1950s and 1960s. While inflation was greatly reduced in the 1980s, productivity and real wage growth showed little recovery from rates experienced during much of the 1970s. For private saving and for federal budget deficits that also influence national saving, however, the major departure from earlier experience took place in the 1980s.

The 1980s were characterized by an extraordinarily low rate of national saving, according to the most widely used measures based on comparisons of current output with resources devoted to consumption. This low national saving rate was produced in part by large federal budget deficits, but it was also accompanied by a significant decline in private saving, both at personal and business levels. Although investment held up quite well, a much larger proportion of investment was financed by borrowing from abroad than was done previously. The inevitable counterpart of extensive borrowing from abroad to finance domestic investment, of course, is a large excess of imports over exports—a large trade deficit.

The combination of a large foreign trade deficit and a sluggish real wage growth contributed to growing concern about the competitiveness of U.S. firms and the productivity of the work force. Although more investment—in physical capital, in new technology, and in the education and training of the work force—is the most promising approach to improving productivity and competitiveness, national fiscal policy and private saving behavior were producing a level of national saving that was extraordinarily low by historical standards and not sufficient to finance domestic investment. There was also little basis to expect that any significant recovery in national saving would emerge to finance a major expansion of investment that could contribute to rising living standards.

Although the domestic investment rate was supported by financing from abroad, the contribution to growth in domestic living standards by such investment would eventually be partially offset by the need for production for export markets to service that larger foreign debt. As long as large federal budget deficits continue to absorb a large share of domestic private saving, national saving will be correspondingly reduced—at least to the degree that federal spending is devoted primarily to supporting higher current individual and collective consumption.

The most recent projections for the federal budget deficit indicate no prospects for significant improvement of the proportion of national output that will need to be devoted to meeting the federal government's borrowing requirements. These prospective fiscal deficits will be incurred during a time when the age distribution of the population foreshadows an obvious prospect—that a much larger share of the national output will need to be devoted to retirement income transfers under the social security retirement program. The federal fiscal outlook points to significant federal government dissaving, at a time when demographic projections imply that national saving and domestically financed current investment should be temporarily high. This would smooth out growth in real income and ensure that real per capita income would continue to increase when the proportion of the population in retirement rises sharply late in the first quarter of the twenty-first century.

Tax Policy and Saving

The large rise in dissaving by the federal government and the marked decline in private saving both contributed to the big drop in national saving in the 1980s. Both are influenced by national tax and fiscal policies, and tax policy changes of various kinds could be considered in an effort to increase national saving.

The sufficiency of revenue to cover current expenditures is one aspect of federal fiscal policy that influences national saving. A shortfall in tax revenues relative to spending—to the extent that federal spending is devoted to consumption instead of investment—contributes directly to lower national saving. The federal budget deficit is an offset to private saving that must be financed by drawing upon private saving or foreign borrowing. Reducing the government's contribution to low national saving requires raising tax revenue, cutting expenditures, or building in trends that move the budget toward closer balance in the future.

A shift in proportions of tax revenue raised from sources with different saving propensities represents a second way in which aggregate saving can be influenced by tax policy. The decline in the proportion of tax revenues raised through personal income taxes and the corresponding rise for the corporate tax share—under the 1986 tax reform act, for example—reduce aggregate saving, because the tax burden was shifted from a low-saving to a high-saving sector. The shift in the share of personal income taxes raised from low-income tax filers to a higher proportion raised from high-income taxpayers also tends to reduce personal saving.

A third way in which tax policy influences saving is through changes in behavior that result from changes in incentives. Motivation

3

for saving is usually presumed to be linked to after-tax returns, which are influenced by tax policy. Although after-tax returns depend both on before-tax returns and on tax policy, they are affected most directly by the tax treatment of saving. In a system based on taxation of income like the U.S. tax system, after-tax returns are in practice influenced primarily through conditions under which vehicles are available for tax-advantaged saving.

Several important links connect the chain of reasoning through which the effects of tax policy on personal saving are analyzed. The most basic issues concern, first, whether personal saving is responsive to real after-tax returns, whether personal saving is positively related to real returns, and if so, what the magnitude of such effects might be. Second, do particular vehicles designed to provide for tax-advantaged savings such as IRAs increase aggregate personal saving, or do they instead mainly influence the composition of saving? An increase in aggregate personal saving might be induced by the direct effects on after-tax returns, but it might also be brought about by promotional efforts, convenience, or modification of saving habits. Finally, from the standpoint of current effects on national saving, is additional personal saving greater than the revenue loss implied by the tax advantage? In principle, this last question should be addressed by comparing the present value of the revenue loss with any additional personal saving instead of using a current cash flow (or five-year budget period) comparison. As a practical matter, however, the credibility of fiscal policy projections for the future may be sufficiently weak that more appropriate, present-value comparisons may be partially discredited.

The distinction between present value and contemporaneous cash flow comparisons is important, because it is pertinent to two different types of tax-advantaged IRA saving vehicles that have been proposed. The so-called front-loaded IRAs—the traditional type in wide use before eligibility was curtailed by the 1986 act—permitted deduction of the amount invested in this manner, within allowable limits, from income subject to the personal income tax. Under these "deductible" IRAs, the cumulative value is subject to taxation when the savings are withdrawn. Back-loaded IRAs, however, permit no immediate deduction from taxable income, but the total value of the accumulated savings is exempted from taxation when the proceeds are withdrawn.

Under simple assumptions the present value of tax revenue losses is equivalent for both kinds of vehicles, as is the value to savers. This equivalence in values, and the conditions under which such equivalence prevails, are described in detail in chapter 8. The timing of the receipt

4

of tax revenues, of course, is very different under the two types of IRAs. The difference in cash-flow tax receipts has important implications for short-term budget projections. In addition, the timing of rewards, as perceived by the typical taxpayer, may significantly influence saving incentives, and this is pointed out in several of the essays in this volume.

Contents of This Volume

In their contributions to this volume, Senator Lloyd Bentsen and Council of Economic Advisers Chairman Michael Boskin both note that domestic investment was financed in significant part during the 1980s by borrowing from abroad, and it must eventually be financed mainly by domestic savings. Both emphasize the importance of investment for growth in the productivity and real incomes of U.S. workers. To encourage domestic personal saving, Senator Bentsen, with his co-sponsor Senator William V. Roth, Jr., proposes expanded IRAs that permit choice between front- or back-loading. From such expanded IRAs, savings could be withdrawn without penalty for initial purchase of a home or for college, as well as for retirement.

Chairman Boskin, after discussing several measurement issues and emphasizing the importance of moving toward a balance in the federal budget, also stresses the importance of increasing personal saving. He argues that the administration's proposed family savings accounts (now called flexible IRAs), a back-loaded variant of IRAs from which savings could be withdrawn without penalty after seven years, would in combination with a number of other tax policy proposals contribute to higher national saving.

John Chapoton and Gregory Ballentine review the politics and economics of the tax changes that were enacted during the 1980s. In their discussion they describe how the reduction in personal income tax rates was accomplished, while increasing or at least not reducing expected tax revenues, by a combination of loophole closing and base broadening and by some shifts in the tax burden. These changes, together with tax-bracket indexation, have exhausted most of the potential for further moves along these lines to raise additional revenue or to grant new tax preferences without reducing revenue.

Rudolph Penner reviews saving trends during the 1970s and 1980s shown by the traditional measures, and he discusses the possible contribution of the growth of the social security retirement program to reduced personal saving. In his discussion of the budget process he describes how the short-term focus of budget decision making can sometimes obstruct changes that would be desirable for the longer term. But he concedes that the somewhat arbitrary consequences of some of the rules intended to constrain spending may be a price that must be paid to restrain, if not reduce, federal government dissaving.

A brief discussion of the history of IRAs is provided by Larry Ozanne. He also describes some of the characteristics of savers who used IRAs, reviews some of the evidence from empirical studies of their influence on saving, and discusses the implications of different features of legislative proposals, such as those for front- or back-loaded IRAs. David Wise summarizes extensive research that he has carried out with Steven Venti that produced evidence that IRAs have achieved the intended result of significantly increasing personal saving. Karl Scholz and William Gale summarize evidence based on their research that challenges this conclusion, and they suggest alternative interpretations of the evidence.

Jonathan Skinner discusses the contradictory conclusions of different assessments of the effects of the IRAs on saving in terms of difficulties that are encountered in efforts to measure substitution between saving through IRAs and through other vehicles. He concludes that IRAs increased personal saving, but he echoes David Wise's view that psychological factors, especially immediate deductibility for front-loaded IRAs, were probably as important as economic incentives.

In the section discussing other goals of tax policy, Joel Slemrod asks why—so soon after the Tax Reform Act of 1986 moved the system toward a broader base, with lower rates and less intrusion into private decision making on resource allocation—most new proposals are oriented toward retreat from those goals. After reviewing the rationale for many reasons for change, he concludes that the basic case for moving toward a low-rate, broad-based system is at least as strong as when these reforms were enacted. Larry Kotlikoff emphasizes the importance of examining the generational impact of tax policy, pointing out that cash-flow based measures of the federal budget deficit do not reflect these effects—primarily because they fail to reflect unfunded liabilities. Wendell Primus focuses on measures of changes in the distribution of income, and in particular on the implications of these changes for children. He points out that the development of methods that permit estimation of broad distributional effects of federal tax and spending programs has heightened the emphasis that will be placed on subjecting tax and other policy changes to an examination of their effects on the distribution of income.

In the final section, intended to place personal saving incentives in the context of national saving objectives, Robert Eisner cautions that we should not be misled by conventional measures of saving, which are subject to serious limitations. Neither should we overlook the potential for more public and private investment to contribute to a more prosperous economy, he argues, that can generate greater saving.

In his discussion of recent saving trends, William Niskanen argues that the case for raising the saving rate rests primarily on the distortion of current policy choices in favor of current instead of deferred consumption—not on recent low saving experience. He questions whether saving performance has deteriorated to the degree shown by conventional measures, and he contends that saving behavior during the 1980s was driven primarily by macroeconomic fiscal effects that produced a sharp rise in real interest rates in the middle of the decade and a dramatic increase in the real value of financial assets.

In Robert Reischauer's view, the slowdown of growth in productivity and living standards since the early 1970s has provided much of the political momentum for changes in tax policy intended to boost productivity growth by stimulating increased saving and investment and for changes intended to redistribute income. After weighing the merit of these approaches, he suggests that focusing increased attention instead on further reducing the federal budget deficit and on increasing investment in human and physical capital are more promising approaches to addressing the underlying problem of improving productivity growth.

Charles Schultze also emphasizes the goal of federal budget deficit reduction as the approach that holds the most promise for raising national saving. He argues that the effectiveness of personal-saving incentives is subject to question and that even after plausible estimates of the indirect costs of higher taxes are taken into account, reducing public dissaving through tax increases remains the most reliable approach to raising national saving from recent levels. These should be regarded as much too low to support a resurgence of productivity growth.

In the concluding chapter of this section, Richard Thaler makes a strong case for reconsidering the way personal saving behavior is conventionally modeled. In his view, households should be viewed as making distinctions among components of their savings, and these distinctions are relevant for their consumption and saving habits. He stresses the importance of saving vehicles that—like traditional, front-loaded IRAs—make saving convenient, provide incentives through rewards that are immediately apparent, and discourage conversion of savings into current consumption.

The essays in this volume are focused mainly on analysis of recent

7

trends in national saving, on the contribution of changes in the federal budget deficit and private saving to these trends, and on incentives to encourage personal saving. Several of these essays are devoted specifically to examination of research evidence that has been developed on the effects of IRAs on personal saving decisions, in view of proposals from both the administration and the Congress to introduce new forms of IRAs and to expand taxpayer eligibility for them. It should be recognized that other tax policy approaches to encourage private saving could be considered, such as, first, expanding private pension opportunities by simplifying procedures for establishing plans, for tax reporting, and for tax-free rollovers; or second, integration of corporate and personal income taxes. In addition, as is emphasized in several of the essays, reducing public-sector dissaving by bringing spending into closer balance with tax revenues may be the most effective way to increase national saving.

PART ONE

Congressional and Executive Branch Perspectives on Tax Policy and Saving

2

Tax Policy and America's Economic Strength

Lloyd Bentsen

As chairman of the Senate Finance Committee, I want to share some ideas about what we can do to encourage saving, to build a stronger and more prosperous American economy, and to create a new era of opportunity for middle-income Americans.

In the Persian Gulf we saw what America could do when it was really committed and had unity of purpose. We proved beyond doubt that there is only one superpower in the world and we are it. That is important because freedom requires that kind of defense.

The Economy and Geopolitics

It is equally important, however, that we remain first not only militarily but also economically. Along those lines we ought to remember several key points. First, the collapse of the Soviet Union has demonstrated that a first class military power cannot be sustained by a third class economy: the economy overloads and then crumbles. To stay the dominant military power in the world, then, America must remain strong economically. Americans must save more, invest more, and produce more efficiently.

Second, military might is by no means the sole determinant of power in the 1990s. The major battles of the future may well be fought over markets and technology, with the Warsaw Pact and NATO taking a back seat to Europe 1992, the Pacific Rim nations, and the North American Free Trade Agreement. Today, we are confident about America's military might but far less confident about the underlying strength

11

of our economy and our ability to compete with the economic forces of the world.

An interesting historical parallel comes to mind. A century ago when America first began to flex its muscles and to extend its power beyond its borders, we stood up to the Europeans, we won a war with Spain, and we acquired an empire. Our country was dynamic; we were emerging but far from being a dominant economic power. England was clearly first. The industrialized nations in Europe failed to realize that America had a weapon that they had failed to consider: a high rate of investment. That factor enabled us to increase our productivity much faster than even England.

Our GNP climbed year after year, eventually surpassing England's. We became first in manufacturing: those savings and investments made it the American century. Of course, our surging population was also important, along with motivated workers, abundant natural resources, a genius for innovation, and free markets. All these played a role then as they still do today.

Nevertheless, a fundamental reason why America prevailed in war and peace, why we were able to create opportunity generation after generation, was our high rate of investment and the soaring increase in productivity. We built a century of power and growth on freedom, hard work, and solid economics.

Today, we are still a dominant economic power, as England was a century ago. Nations like Japan, Germany, and South Korea, however, are closing that gap by outsaving, outinvesting, and outproducing America. Nowhere is it written in stone that we will forever remain number one as an economic power. That title is not hereditary but has to be earned with commitment, discipline, and wise management, qualities often lacking in America lately.

During the 1980s, we lost leadership in key areas of technology and ran massive trade deficits year after year. We became the number-one debtor nation in the world and exported millions of high-paying manufacturing jobs. Our national debt quadrupled, and in 1991 each American family paid $1,500 in taxes just to service the debt incurred since 1981.

How did we manage during this time? We sold off assets and held down wages so that the manufacturing wage in this country today is less than that of some of our major competitors like West Germany. Paradoxically, however, the salaries of management and of CEOs of manufacturing companies increased to 118 times the wage of the average factory

12

worker. In Japan the salary of top management is 18 times the salary of the average factory worker.

We borrowed from abroad, from nations like Japan and Germany, and foreign capital made up for our decade of lack of savings. Today, that equation of dependence has changed dramatically, creating a credit crunch in our country. Foreign investment is declining, from $71 billion in 1989 to $37 billion in 1990, a decrease of almost 50 percent.

Much of the German money that was coming here is now going into East Germany. In addition, the Japanese are now investing in their infrastructure.

The Deficit

We have been hearing for years that high levels of foreign investment in this country show the strength of our economy and the world's confidence in our economy. Now I wonder about the other side of that argument. As we see that investment decline, do we suppose that confidence in our economic future is waning? Clearly, the dramatic reduction in foreign investment requires us to compensate. One of the obvious ways to adjust is to increase our own saving and investment and, of course, to keep pressure on the government, on Congress, and on the administration to reduce that deficit in the budget.

The deficit reduction agreement in 1990 produced the tightest constraints ever put on an administration and a Congress. Although the negotiations were as difficult as any I have ever been involved in, the democratic process worked, and we finally cobbled together something that will tightly control federal spending.

The deficit monster, however, is also stalking the states and local jurisdictions. If we do see any recovery, it will be muddled and slow in the process. We will not have the kind of fiscal stimulant from the government that we have seen in the past.

We have continuing deficit pressures, with cuts in programs important to America. With foreign investment declining, capital shortages are getting worse at a time when our economy urgently requires substantial investment in new factories to increase our productivity.

Japan, for example, with a population one-third smaller than our own, outinvested America dollar for dollar in 1989. Last year, Japan's investment was 30 percent higher than our own. Its savings rate was 16 percent in comparison with our 4 percent. It deploys twice as much capital per worker as we do. Japanese productivity year in and year out grows two-and-a-half times faster than ours, and if the present trend

13

continues, Japan's GNP per capita will exceed ours early in the next century.

Japan is by no means our only major credible competitor for economic leadership in the world. In a few years, Europe with a population and an economy comparable with ours will be united. Even now many of the workers are earning more per capita than our own.

While those trends are serious, they do not tell the whole story. They do not demonstrate how the excesses of the 1980s robbed middle-income Americans of hope and opportunity.

That period was hard on many Americans. Working men and women with families saw their real annual wages decrease by $190 a year, and yet the cost of a college education in real terms went up 88 percent. For the first time since World War II, home ownership declined. Millions of young American couples who wanted to be on their own moved in with their families: the median cost of a home had gone up by some 56 percent. Car prices nearly tripled.

More and more Americans worked harder and longer hours than ever before to try to keep from falling behind. Two paychecks became a necessity. The number of working mothers increased by 50 percent. More women were working both numerically and as a percentage than had worked during World War II in the days of "Rosie the riveter." The amount of time that parents could spend parenting dropped by about 40 percent.

Despite all this extra effort, the reward for middle-income families proved meager. While their income increased by 3 percent during the 1980s, it had increased by 15 percent during the 1970s. How did these families manage? They managed by dissaving, by borrowing so heavily on the equity in their homes that in many cases the debt outran the value of the home, causing family wealth to sink during the decade.

Dissaving is obviously not a long-term solution. It is reminiscent of the story about the man who trained the horse not to eat and then complained that the horse died just as it learned the trick. We cannot continue to sweep the economic problems of this country under the rug. We cannot continue to blink at the signs of distress and hope for the best or indulge in narrow partisan rankling or one-upmanship when designing economic policy.

Individual Retirement Accounts

America needs the same kind of courage, decisiveness, commitment, and unity that worked so well in the Persian Gulf. I would like to see

14

these qualities in Congress, in the administration, and in the American public. All of us need to understand the seriousness of the situation.

What can we do together to strengthen this economy of ours, to build for the future, and to respond to the deepest concerns of middle-income America, concerns like home ownership, health care, education, and a secure retirement? A good place to start might be to enact the Bentsen-Roth individual retirement account (IRA) for all working Americans.

This idea makes sense for America. It has been endorsed by 77 members of the U.S. Senate and by 237 members of the House, both Republicans and Democrats, both liberals and conservatives. Why does the Bentsen-Roth IRA have that kind of support? The American people understand it, and they like it; the IRA stimulates savings and empowers people to plan for their future.

Bringing the IRA out of retirement is something we can do now to jump-start savings and help millions of working Americans plan for tomorrow. We propose a choice of IRAs, either the traditional front-end IRA, where the individual takes a $2,000 deduction going in, or as an alternative an IRA that is not deductible but that allows the contributor to pay no taxes on the earnings during the period the money is held in that account.

That proposal has been criticized on two counts. First, it will be expensive: for the short run, the critics are right; but my reply is, "We'll pay for it." Second, some critics claim that IRAs do not really create new savings, that the rich are simply shifting their savings. Here the critics are wrong: the personal saving rate was higher when the fully deductible IRA was in place from 1982 to 1986 than it has been since. Indeed, personal savings fell to a postwar low the year after IRAs were restricted in the name of tax reform. Several studies have looked into the source of IRA funds and concluded that fully two-thirds came from new savings. I expect that issue will be debated more fully today, but IRAs certainly create a significant increase in savings that otherwise would not have taken place. And it is indisputable that our economy desperately needs the additional capital.

A psychological factor is also at work in IRAs. Some economists believe that high-profile instruments such as the IRA produce a recognition effect that creates a general appreciation for savings. How does the choice affect a taxpayer when he sits down to write out that check on April 15—does he write it to the IRS, or does he write it to the IRA and put it in his own savings account? The fact that our plan allows a contributor to withdraw from an IRA without a penalty to buy a first home or pay for college or a serious illness, as well as retirement, will attract additional savers.

Obviously, this plan is not some magical elixir that will solve all our problems. Alone, it will not solve our trade problems or our deficit problems. It will not educate or inoculate our children. It will not erase the results of a decade of indulgence. But it will help; it will encourage millions of Americans to save, and it will help individual families plan for an uncertain future.

There is no reason why Americans should shrink from that uncertainty. We have always welcomed challenge. We have always assumed that problems could be solved, and in America we have solved more than our fair share of them. While we have plenty of problems—trade, savings, consumption, taxes, education, health insurance—let us not forget that America has assets that are the envy of the rest of the world. We have not just military strength but the strength of a free people committed to a free market system. We have an enduring commitment to private enterprise that is the backbone of our prosperity in this country. For more than two centuries, America has set the standard for freedom and opportunity. Millions of people have endured incredible hardships to come to these shores, to be a part of the American experience.

When I was in Denmark not long ago—I am of Danish ancestry—I was talking to the American ambassador to Denmark. He said, "Senator, I guess you're over here looking at all your ancestral castles." I said, "Let me tell you something, Mr. Ambassador. If my family had castles, they would never have left this place." That's the way it is with almost all of us—there are not many kings and queens in our genes.

But I will tell you something we do have and that we share in those genes: we are risk takers, people who are ready to take on the odds, leave families, friends, and languages we understand to come to a new country for a chance for a step up in life. An English writer over here a hundred years ago referred to Americans as "by nature optimists." He said, "Nowhere else in the world does an individual associate himself more constantly and directly with the greatness of his country."

Today, we are being challenged to preserve the greatness of our country and the future of our people. We have it in our power to respond to that challenge, to build a future as proud as our past. We cannot guarantee the success of every American, and we should not try. But we can join hands to create pathways and provide incentives that encourage private enterprise and enable the American people to seize control of their own destiny.

16

3

Fiscal Policy, Saving, and Economic Growth

Michael J. Boskin

Today I will address the critical subject of saving and the forces that affect saving behavior, and will then move on to investment, productivity growth, and fiscal policy. My focus will primarily be on the long-run evolution of the economy and saving rates averaged over many years or decades, rather than on the current, short-term behavior of the economy.

Saving

Saving is of fundamental importance for individual families or households because it enables them to transfer resources across time and across what economists call states of the world, defined by various risks that individuals, households, industries, and economies face. Saving also finances productive investment, which is one of the sources of increasing national wealth, productivity growth, expanded gross national product (GNP), and a higher standard of living in the future.

In a purely closed economy, the same type of saving would play all of these roles. Since we live in a world where capital flows rapidly across international boundaries in substantial volume, however, the link between domestic saving and domestic investment is broken. But I believe it will stay broken only for a finite amount of time and a finite amount of saving.

I do not believe that an advanced economy such as that of the United States or any other major country can rely indefinitely on foreign capital inflows for a large fraction of its gross national product to finance a major share of its domestic investment. Ultimately, the domestic

17

investment rate in a country will be constrained. Perhaps this will occur over the span of a decade rather than a few years. But it will be constrained by the available supply of domestic saving.

Domestic investment, of course, is important as a source of productivity growth, because it directly increases the amount of capital available per worker and indirectly affects the rate at which new technology is diffused throughout the economy.

If learning-by-doing models are correct, or if it is preferable for cost or technological reasons to embody new technology in new capital as opposed to old capital, then the rate of technical innovation and ensuing productivity growth will indeed depend on the rate of investment.

Economic growth may sound like an abstraction, but a difference of only one percentage point or even half a percentage point in annual economic growth over a decade makes an enormous difference to the success or failure of a society's economy.

Our understanding of productivity growth as a profession and as a society leaves an immense amount to be desired. But we do know that productivity growth is not something that falls like manna from heaven, totally independent of economic conditions or economic policy. It heavily reflects fiscal policy, monetary and regulatory policies, and trade regimes.

Therefore, saving is critically important because it does not just represent a stockpile of money for a rainy day or for retirement. Saving is essential for financing, investment, and productivity growth, which every society depends upon to remain vital and prosperous.

How high should our saving rate be? Is the current rate an appropriate one? Why has it declined in recent years?

Most economists are familiar with the argument that we ought to let the private sector make these decisions. In the absence of any external benefits, costs, or preexisting distortions to those markets, the argument goes, the free market forces of saving and investing should lead to the private sector's making socially optimal decisions.

In reality, we have a large number of distortions in our economy. They stem from the double taxation of saving inherent in a taxation of income when there is no fully allowable, tax-deferred saving at the margin. They stem from a very large drain on private resources that federal budgets entail if and when they are not fully offset by private saving.

The federal government also affects saving through regulation of financial markets. The Bush administration's banking reform proposals are enormously important for generating and channeling saving into its most productive uses, and for ensuring that our financial system will be efficient as we enter the twenty-first century. If we continue to require our financial institutions to do business under archaic regulations that date back to the Great Depression, we risk losing a large number of those transactions to markets overseas. These archaic regulations are just one example of the way the government distorts saving decisions through regulation, taxation, and the government's net fiscal position.

Speaking of fiscal position, let me quickly address the issue of budget deficits. There are some economists who argue that budget deficits do not matter. Others contend that budget deficits are the only things that matter, and that the structure of the tax system or the composition of federal spending does not affect the economy.

I view each of these positions as extreme and incorrect. Deficits—and expected future deficits—do matter. Deficits have a large cumulative impact over time on national saving, and therefore on the economy's long-run growth potential.

Measuring Saving Behavior

There are an enormous number of conceptual and measurement problems in understanding saving behavior in a complex economy like that of the United States. The Commerce Department usually estimates saving as a residual by subtracting consumption from income. But every time we incorrectly estimate income or consumption, we potentially cause large measurement errors in saving.

There is also a serious issue concerning the level of aggregation one ought to examine. One could look at the saving done by the private sector, including households and business firms, or at the net position of the federal, state, and local government's surplus or deficit, or at national saving, or at the sum of all these. There is also a conceptual difference and debate pertaining to whether net saving or gross saving is the accurate measure.

In my view, looking at the total saving for the nation is probably the best place to start, but it is not sufficient by itself. Various aspects of credit markets indicate a need to understand corporate cash flow and its effect on investment. Therefore, I would also include business saving and personal saving separately in a complete assessment of saving.

Concerning net versus gross, a large fraction of the decline in the net saving rate in the United States is due to the rise in capital consumption. Capital consumption allowances as a share of GNP in the

19

1980s were 1.2 percentage points higher than they were in the 1950s and 1960s.

Are we measuring that depreciation appropriately? Are we getting at true economic depreciation? Should we consider that replacement capital as well as the net addition to the capital stock embodies new technology?

These issues are sometimes sloughed off by economists running a regression, doing a study, or deriving a statistic. But there is a richer set of answers available, which will enable us to better understand the economy, if we look at several of the components in the disaggregated nature of saving as well as aggregate levels of gross national saving or real net saving.

While saving in the United States is substantially higher than the typical Commerce Department figures reveal when one takes a more comprehensive view, including such items as consumer durables, it is incontrovertible that saving by any measure has declined substantially in the United States. As is less well known, saving has declined substantially in virtually every major country in the world in the 1980s relative to the 1970s.

Net saving declined on the National Economic Accounts basis to about 2.1 percent of GNP in 1990, from approximately 7 to 8 percent in the 1960s. If we disaggregate that figure we see that a larger fraction of the decline was in private saving rather than in the rise of the combined federal, state, and local deficit. The enormous increase in net capital consumption accounts for a large share of the decline in private saving.

Real and Nominal Investment

There is another statistic that is not often appreciated but is certainly important when we discuss the 1980s. Real investment has been substantially higher than nominal investment as a share of GNP in the United States. This is partly the result of the improvement in measurement that has been made in capital goods deflators. If you spend $10,000 on a computer today, you will buy an immensely larger amount of computing power than you would have bought by spending the same amount several years ago. The price of computing, as opposed to computers, has declined substantially. In this respect, we are now getting more capital value.

Many observers noticed that the nominal investment rate fell substantially in the 1980s. These same observers complained that we imported a lot of foreign capital and then purportedly consumed it all. This brings up a serious issue involved in looking at these data, and one can tell a very different story from looking at real investment rather than nominal investment. Real investment in the 1980s was high by historical standards, rather than low. The current three-percentage point difference between real investment as a share of real GNP and nominal investment as a share of nominal GNP happens to be roughly equivalent to the average net import of foreign capital for a large part of the 1980s.

I want to underline the vital importance that productivity growth plays in the future course of our nation, pertaining not only to our domestic economy but to our role in the world community as well. Investment is an enormously important component of higher productivity growth; ultimately we will have to finance our own investment.

As I mentioned earlier, we are still distorting many of the choices that are made with budget deficits and with our tax, regulatory, and other systems. It is my conclusion that we must focus on raising our national saving rate to reach the level it would be were it not for government-imposed distortions. It would be appropriate to start with a goal of achieving a national saving rate several percentage points higher than it is now.

How do we do that? The first and surest way to increase the national saving rate is to decrease the federal government's borrowing, so long as it is not done in a way that decreases private saving, holding constant the path of GNP.

A tremendous disjuncture currently exists between the measured budget deficit and a measure that is economically relevant to macroeconomics and to credit markets. Economists have long known that deficits rise and fall with economic conditions, so it is common to distinguish between a structural deficit and a cyclical deficit. A modest portion of the deficits in 1991 and 1992 were due to the recession.

Savings and Loan Costs

A much larger issue is the savings and loan costs. Deposit insurance outlays in 1990 approximated $60 billion, and are expected to be larger for a year or two before declining.

Eventually we will have paid off all the depositors, all the failed savings and loans will be closed, and deposit insurance will be cleaned up. Therefore, the outlay should be seen as a transitory one—very large, but lasting perhaps only two or three years. Much of the outlay in the short term represents working capital, a large fraction of which will, we hope, get returned in the out years. The need for working capital occurs because, after acquiring assets from failed savings and loans, the Resolution Trust Corporation (RTC) typically holds on to the asset for awhile, rather than turning it over instantaneously.

There is disagreement about the exact size of the ultimate savings and loan cost and about the timing of the resolution. But there is very little macroeconomic significance as to whether an extra $10 billion or $15 billion is borrowed to support savings and loans. I think thoughtful economists from all areas of the spectrum would agree with this.

The serious confidence issue pertaining to the savings and loan system has a large potential impact on the economy. Therefore, whether we pay a little bit more or a little bit less for the bailout, it is critical that we pay off the depositors who were insured and who expected to get their funds replaced.

Let me give you an example. Rudy Penner made a small deposit at an S & L that "went under" in the Washington, D.C. area. Rudy's money was replaced within a day. Rudy had no reason to change his spending patterns. He expected that he had his money, and indeed the government borrowed the money to cover his account; and the money was redeposited in the financial sector, so it was a net wash in credit markets. This is an argument I know most of you are familiar with.

Deficits

Deficits are still a serious problem, even though the economically relevant deficit is probably the NIPA structural deficit, not the one we hear most about in the media.

When we finally get over the "hump" caused by the S & L outlays and borrowing, and when the NIPA structural deficit heads toward zero, an important question will remain: Should we ultimately be running consolidated budget surpluses? Over a span of time longer than typical economic fluctuations, we probably have good reason to be running at least modest surpluses in the government, to prepare to expand the resources for the baby boom generation's retirement.

I believe that we will also have to revisit some parts of our tax structure. This administration has proposed restoring a capital gains differential; family savings accounts that are carefully designed to minimize the up-front budget cost to the federal government, enabling

22

people to save on a tax-free basis for retirement as well as for preretirement objectives; and such other tax features as making the research and experimentation tax credit permanent.

We want to keep tax rates low and to keep a relatively stable tax structure that people can depend and plan on. We certainly do not need anything like a massive overhaul, such as we had in 1986 or 1981.

Some specific areas in the tax code will need to be addressed in the short and the long run. Over the long term we will need to revisit issues of double taxation of dividends and the tax bias against equity.

In my view, the experiment that was run in the 1980s with IRAs is often misrepresented in its impact. There was a lot going on in saving in the 1980s. Although evidence is certainly not conclusive, those who say that IRAs did not work to stimulate saving because the saving rate fell in the 1980s are not asking the right question.

The right question is, "What would the saving rate have been had we not had IRAs in the 1980s?" My conclusion is that IRAs did raise saving relative to what it would have been in their absence. Part of the reason for the decline in the personal saving rate in the 1980s can be attributed to things that were going on almost automatically in pension funds.

In summary, the issues of saving, consumption, and tax policy are of paramount importance. They will determine the long-run evolution of our society and our future success economically as a nation and as a leader of the free world.

PART TWO

The Political Economy of
Tax Policy in the 1980s

4

The Tortuous Route to
Tax Rate Reduction

John E. Chapoton

After some thirty years in the tax business, including two stints in the Office of Tax Policy at the Treasury Department, I think I know something about the structure of the tax system; but I question whether anybody can be certain of the policy goals of our tax code. Obviously, the system is designed to accomplish more than just raising revenues. It is a vehicle for implementing broad policy goals. But those goals, and the methods by which the tax system seeks to implement them, can shift dramatically over the years.

The Evolving Tax System

The 1980s offer a good example—almost a controlled experiment—of the shifts in policy goals reflected in the tax system. There is some truth in the standard Washington line, "What goes around comes around." We may now be witnessing a new shift in tax policy, different from anything we saw in the 1980s.

In the late 1970s and early 1980s, a major tax policy issue was the overtaxation of corporate America by the understatement of depreciation deductions. High inflation caused cost recovery deductions to be understated, and thus taxable income was overstated. This, of course, was particularly burdensome for the capital-intensive industries in this country.

At the same time there was much talk about the need to do something to make American companies more competitive in the world marketplace. The Internal Revenue Code was considered an ideal

27

instrument for addressing this problem: a vehicle to reverse the decline in productivity of corporate America.

A related concern was the low U.S. saving rate. It was compared then, as it is today, with the very high saving rate in Japan, and it was thought that the tax code was the culprit, or at least that through the tax code something could be done about it.

President Reagan's 1980 campaign focused on these problems, and his first legislative initiative as president, announced on February 18, 1981, was the Economic Recovery Program, which relied primarily on proposed tax changes. It consisted of a two-pronged tax program: first, a greatly accelerated cost recovery system for corporations, and second, of course, dramatic individual rate reductions—the most visible feature of the supply-side theory. The president originally proposed a 30 percent reduction in tax rates across the board; Congress ultimately enacted a 25 percent slash in rates.

The business community lined up solidly behind the program, even though the form of the corporate tax relief—increased depreciation deductions and investment tax credits—benefited almost entirely the capital-intensive industries. Such industries as the service industries, the financial services community, high-tech companies, and retailers received very little benefit from the accelerated cost recovery program, but they all got behind President Reagan's tax program in toto—even though it meant that their corporate tax rate would stay at 46 percent.

Corporate America subscribed to the argument that the program would rejuvenate an economy caught in the vise of high inflation and low productivity. The seduction of dramatically lower individual tax rates was also a very enticing benefit for the decision makers in the business community. In any event, they were unified in support of President Reagan's program in 1981.

So much political support was given to these goals from both sides of the aisle in 1981 that the issue soon became not whether to enact this type of tax benefit, but whether it was enough. Indeed, the Ways and Means Committee, which was certainly not known as a pro-business body, responded to the Reagan program not by disparaging it but by designing an alternative set of accelerated depreciation provisions that were just as generous as the Reagan administration's fifteen–ten–five–three proposal.

The Reagan administration had originally proposed only the two-pronged tax program—cost recovery benefits for business and lower tax rates for individuals. But political support for other tax benefits—most of them sold as incentives for saving and investment, or to increase the work incentive of individuals, or to increase the productivity of corporations—was so overwhelming that in June 1981 the Reagan administration adopted as its own a broad range of additional tax benefits.

One such add-on was the 25 percent credit for research and experimentation. Others included generous credits for rehabilitation of real estate, the universal IRA, and a special deduction for two-earner families.

There were also some bizarre proposals, such as the All Saver Certificate. In 1981 you could deposit a limited amount in a savings and loan or a bank and the earnings would be tax free for a year or two. It was supposed to increase savings.

The 1981 tax act also introduced indexation of the individual tax rates and the personal exemption into our tax law. This was a very important innovation in tax policy. The Reagan administration initially required much prodding from Capitol Hill, but it soon became a great champion of indexation. Although the law was enacted in 1981, the effective date of indexing was deferred until 1985.

The administration also proposed and designed the popular and short-lived safe-harbor leasing provision. The Treasury Department was greatly concerned about the fact that the new and generous accelerated cost recovery benefits could not be utilized by corporations that did not have current tax liability. Thus a significant disparity in the after-tax cost of plant and equipment would be created between companies and between industries. So safe-harbor leasing, designed to make traditional leasing transactions more efficient, was proposed by Treasury and adopted by the Congress.

It was, of course, repealed within a year. The idea of a fictional transaction to transfer tax benefits appeared fraudulent to the public. So we returned to traditional tax leasing, in which the middleman rakes off more of the profit. Although not as effective, this approach was more easily understood.

The ink was barely dry on the Economic Recovery Tax Act (ERTA) in 1981 when the administration and Capitol Hill began to face the stark reality of what a $750 billion tax cut over five years would mean. Squeezed by the commencement of indexing in 1985, the new tax code meant that government could no longer rely on bracket creep to increase tax revenues quietly, without legislation. So the focus in the tax world began to change and to change immediately—as early as the fall of 1981. The focus shifted to the need for additional revenues from the tax system.

The 1981 tax bill narrowed the tax base and, of course, lowered individual tax rates. All subsequent bills in the 1980s broadened the tax base. The primary goal of each of the subsequent bills—in 1982, 1983, 1984, 1986, 1987, 1988, and 1989—was to broaden the tax base. The Tax Equality and Fiscal Responsibility Act (TEFRA) of 1982, the Social Security Bill of 1983 (which broadened the tax base by including a part of social security receipts in taxable income) and the Deficit Reduction Act (DEFRA) accomplished significant base broadening.

Every bill except the Tax Reform Act of 1986 used the additional revenue raised from base broadening to reduce the deficit. The 1986 act followed the same technique as the other bills, except that all of the revenue was used to reduce rates across the board, both individual and corporate rates. But the philosophy and the purpose were the same throughout the remainder of the 1980s. After significant reduction of the tax base—particularly the corporate tax base—in 1981, we switched entirely: in subsequent years, base broadening was the tax policy goal. Of course, it was not always referred to as base-broadening. The sales pitch varied from year to year.

In 1982 the rhetoric emphasized the need to improve fairness by closing loopholes and collecting taxes that were already due but were not being collected because of inadequate enforcement tools in the law. The base-broadening aspects of the 1982 act were quite significant. It straightforwardly revoked part of the depreciation deductions that had been adopted in 1981. It also repealed safe-harbor leasing; tightened the industrial development bond rules for private purpose tax-exempt financing; restructured the completed contract method of accounting; and imposed a 15 percent across-the-board cut in corporate tax preferences. For individuals, the 1982 act adopted a very tough alternative minimum tax, put limits on medical expense and casualty deductions, and adopted tax withholding for interest and dividends, which was itself repealed about eight months later.

The 1982 act was marketed and sold as a loophole closing, not as a tax increase. It was so described by the administration and by Congress. But in fact it was simply an attempt to raise revenue without enacting legislation that had to be labeled as a tax increase. And it did raise revenue: it raised more than $200 billion over the five-year budget period.

The Deficit Reduction Act of 1984 was a carbon copy of the 1982 act. It had the same policy goals and the same political goals: tax increases by base broadening without raising the rates; tax base broadening that could reasonably be called loophole closing or more effective

30

IRS enforcement techniques. But politically it had to be called anything other than a tax increase.

Substantively the provisions were very similar to the provisions adopted in 1982, but they were much harder to achieve from a political standpoint because the easy targets had been dealt with in the earlier bill. Thus the 1984 bill was a much more comprehensive piece of legislation, with each provision having a smaller base-broadening effect. To raise significant revenue with less dramatic changes the bill had to contain more numerous changes affecting many more taxpayers.

The 1984 act contained voluminous tax accounting changes—requiring capitalization of prepaid expenses, capitalization of start-up expenses, capitalization of principal and interest during construction of buildings, tightening of the original issue discount rules, tightening of the market discount rules, and all sorts of anti-abuse, reformist provisions affecting corporations and partnerships.

In the individual area, there were both significant new restrictions in the pension rules and a number of anti-abuse provisions dealing with partnerships and compensation devices. The 1984 act was an extremely large tax bill. As each of the successive base-broadening tax bills after 1981 was enacted, the specific tax law changes became more painful to adopt and the bills got larger. ERTA, the 1981 tax bill, amended or added 483 sections of the Internal Revenue Code; TEFRA in 1983 amended or added 530 sections of the Internal Revenue Code; DEFRA in 1984 amended or added 2,245 sections of the Internal Revenue Code; and the 1986 act amended or added 2,704 sections of the Internal Revenue Code. It is not hard to see why the professionals giving tax advice have had an interesting time in the 1980s.

Political Impacts

During the years that followed the 1981 act the politics of tax legislation was going through an interesting evolution. The increased investment incentives adopted in 1981 had given a huge boost to the tax shelter industry; many corporations and individuals were able to reduce their taxes to little or nothing. Those investment incentives and the related safe-harbor lease debacle reopened discussions of the fairness of the tax code; issues of fairness and equity had not really appeared in the tax debates of 1981.

For example, it was disclosed in 1983 that the so-called Generals—General Motors, General Dynamics, and General Electric—had paid no tax for several years. Indeed, General Dynamics had not paid any taxes since 1974. Such disclosures were not without political impact.

In addition, a split had developed in the corporate community. While the capital-intensive industries had a very low tax burden, the rest of corporate America was left holding the bag—they still paid a 46 percent corporate tax rate. It began to dawn on them that they were the stepchildren of the tax system.

Coalitions of so-called high-tax companies were formed and became very active in the tax legislative struggles of 1982 and 1984. They did not argue that their taxes should be reduced but that if taxes had to be increased—and all knowledgeable observers saw that tax increases were going to occur—the burden of such a tax increase should be shifted from them to other corporate taxpayers who had enjoyed the lion's share of the tax benefits passed out in 1981. So the political discussion was changing.

I gave a talk in early 1984 in which I discussed the tax policy issues affecting businesses, and I pointed out that the ground was shifting:

> In any event, the fact is that the burden of double taxation of corporate earnings has been decreased and decreased dramatically, to the point that the broad corporate tax issue of today is no longer integration of the corporate and individual income taxes as it was in the middle 1970s. The broad corporate issue of today instead is the treatment of unused or unusable tax benefits and NOL carryovers, as well as leasing transactions, mergers, and spinoffs, all of which are designed to ensure maximum use of tax benefits accruing from capital investment.
>
> The dilemma we find ourselves in is that the cost of new capital equipment is significantly higher when the cost recovery and interest deductions cannot be fully utilized. Thus, the true after-tax cost of plant and equipment varies tremendously from industry to industry and from company to company within an industry.
>
> ACRS and its predecessors did not solve the problem; they exacerbated it. Our tinkering with the cost recovery allowances over the years may well have left us in the worst of worlds from an efficiency standpoint: high marginal tax rates on corporate income (46 percent), with the disincentive effects high marginal rates can cause; and low effective tax rates, but rates that vary widely from industry to industry.
>
> The need to deal with excess tax losses without substantially increasing the tax burden on invested capital and the need to equalize effective tax rates across industry lines are

considerations that ought to drive fundamental tax reform in the corporate area, once it has been decided how large a role the corporate tax should play on the receipt side of the budget. Perhaps the better approach would be a decrease in cost recovery benefits and, at the same time, a reduction in corporate tax rates across the board.

During this time President Reagan delivered his 1984 State of the Union message, in which he said he had directed Secretary Donald Regan to develop a plan for fundamental tax reform at the Treasury Department. The plan was, in fact, developed at Treasury during 1984, without the White House knowing even its basic thrust. Reflecting the shift in thinking among tax policy makers following 1981, the Treasury plan called for massive base broadening at both the corporate and individual levels, with the resulting revenue increase being used to reduce tax rates.

Tax neutrality, the absence of tax incentives, removal of taxes as a consideration from economic decision making—these became the buzz words in 1985 and 1986. They fed on themselves as the legislative process built and shaped the 1986 act. The effect was that any code provision affecting or tilting economic decision making was suspect. This was true of even the most visible and popular tax incentives. The Individual Retirement Account, a classic example, fell to the ax of base broadening and decreasing individual rates.

This same trend continued in 1987 and 1988. Moreover, we are now seeing more discussion of equity and fairness; the distribution of the tax burden across income classes has come to center stage. It was clearly the factor that defeated President Bush's proposal for a cut in the tax on capital gains in 1991.

The same arguments may move the tax rates up if revenue is needed either for low income relief or, ironically, for saving incentives. And there is increased interest among policy makers in tax incentives designed to increase personal saving or to influence business investment toward job-creating plants and equipment; the pendulum is swinging back. It is obvious that we are once again witnessing a shift in the political rhetoric that surrounds the discussion of taxes.

5

Tax Policy and
Revenue Sufficiency in the 1980s

J. Gregory Ballentine

All the tax bills subsequent to the 1981 tax act broadened the tax base in fairly similar ways. Generally they broadened the corporate tax base or, where the individual income tax base was broadened, they altered provisions affecting high-income individuals or the investment incomes of individuals.

Base-Broadening Provisions

That regularity is the background for my evaluation of our tax structure and how it meets our goals today. That amounts to an evaluation of the 1986 act, which has not changed substantially since it was enacted. The 1986 act broadened the tax base in ways similar to those of the 1982 and 1984 acts, but it used the resulting revenues to lower tax rates rather than to lower the deficit. I will evaluate the impact of current tax laws (the 1986 act) on saving, but I will not restrict my focus to private saving; indeed, I am going to stress the impact on national saving.

Any evaluation of the structure of our tax system today should specify which alternative system it is contrasted against. Some contrasts are made against a pure income tax system or a pure consumption tax system. That is an interesting academic exercise, but not relevant as a practical matter because pure systems are rarely of any political feasibility.

The more natural comparison that analysts tend to make of the 1986 act—the tax law today—is with the pre-1986 law. The comparison effectively assumes that had the 1986 act not occurred, the tax law would not have changed from what it was in 1986.

That is a natural context, but it is misleading. The law that existed in 1986 was part of a continuing evolution and was quite unlikely to have remained as it was. The context in which I will evaluate the 1986 act is relative to the system we would have had, had we not broadened the base to cut individual and corporate income tax rates in 1986. I believe that, without the 1986 act, many of the base-broadening provisions of that act would have been used later to raise revenues.

Obviously, many will disagree with this view. The base-broadening provisions in 1986 were not different in kind from those used in 1982 and 1984 to raise revenues. Some of them were larger, certainly. The full repeal of the investment tax credit had a much greater effect on revenues and effective marginal tax rates than what was done to the investment tax credit in 1982—half basis adjustment for the investment tax credit. In the type of their effect, however, repeal of the investment tax credit and basis adjustment are very similar—they both restrict the up-front investment incentive for purchases of equipment.

The largest class of base-broadening provisions in the 1986 act, after the repeal of the investment tax credit, was provisions that essentially took the language of the 1982 bill having to do with the completed contract accounting method and applied it to many other types of business activities, particularly inventories.

My view is that had we not had the 1986 act we would have continued to have bills like those of 1982 and 1984, using many of the base-broadening provisions of the 1986 act that were similar to those of 1984 and 1982 to reduce revenues. Of course we had tax increases after 1986, but they were small compared with those of 1982 and 1984. A major reason why the 1987 and later tax bills were so small is that many of the most politically acceptable base-broadening provisions were used in 1986 to reduce tax rates.

President Reagan's "Make my day" and President Bush's "Read my lips" led many to conclude that tax increases were not politically possible, independent of the 1986 act. A brief review of certain historical actions as opposed to rhetoric, however, may alter that view.

In September 1981, soon after the 1981 tax bill had been enacted, President Reagan announced on national television that there would be need for revenue enhancement. That was when the term "revenue enhancement" was first made public. It was not a term created by a Democratic Congress, but rather one used by the White House to describe tax increases that were not perceived by the voting public as tax increases: that is, base-broadening provisions of the type enacted in 1982, 1984, and 1986.

The fact sheet associated with the president's address described several base-broadening provisions supported by the administration. In the president's budget a few months later, the list had grown. Those provisions, along with others, were later enacted in the Tax Equity and Fiscal Responsibility Act of 1982 (TEFRA), which was supported by the administration.

In 1984, while President Reagan was running against Walter Mondale, he argued that Mondale was going to raise voters' taxes and he, Reagan, would not. During the campaign, however, in August 1984, President Reagan signed the second largest permanent income tax increase in our history. But it was not perceived as having raised taxes. Why not? Because it was largely composed of base-broadening provisions of the same kind that were used in TEFRA and were to appear again in 1986.

After the Treasury's tax reform proposal was brought over to the White House in 1986, the *Wall Street Journal* published an interview with President Reagan about that proposal. The interviewer asked the president how he was able to support the very large corporate tax increase in that proposal. The president responded that there was no corporate tax increase in the proposal, that in fact the corporate tax rate was reduced. The interviewer pointed out that, while the corporate tax rate was reduced in the proposal, corporate taxes were increased by about $25 billion a year. The president indicated that he did not know that and would have to look into it. Apparently the president's investigation led him to believe that base-broadening corporate tax increases were acceptable.

A lot of evidence shows that an administration whose rhetoric was strongly against raising taxes could consistently accept base-broadening tax provisions that could be described as eliminating obsolete incentives, closing abuses, leveling the playing field, and making the tax system more neutral. The 1986 act made it more difficult for this to be continued, however. First, it used up many of the remaining politically viable options for base broadening. Second, it was apparently based on an implicit agreement not to engage in substantial income tax changes for some time.

It is informative to evaluate the tax system we have, and the enactment of the 1986 act, in comparison with a system that would have used many of the act's base-broadening provisions to raise revenues. An example of the alternative that I use for this comparison might have begun in 1987. During the first nine months of that year the administration opposed any tax increase. After the stock market crash in October the administration decided that a budget deal that included some taxes was acceptable. The result was a very small tax increase. If some of the base-broadening provisions used in 1986 had still been available, a larger tax increase might have been acceptable.

Rate Reductions and Saving

Using this context, what is my evaluation? I will focus on the impact on saving, but first I will mention a couple of the other factors. One criterion of a tax system that economists do not look at as much as they should is the complexity of the tax system and what impact that has on the economy. Although the 1986 law as a technical document is quite complex, it will lead to much greater stability compared with the continual changes that would have occurred without the 1986 act. Since change itself has been the major source of tax complexity, this stability of the 1986 act is a great virtue.

Equity is always a difficult matter to evaluate. The evolutionary process against which I am contrasting the 1986 act would not have had the individual rate reductions of that act. Therefore the particular rate reductions that affected low-income persons and labor income would have been lost. Many would view that as a disadvantage of having the evolutionary system instead of the 1986 act.

Another impact of the rate reductions, however, is not so equitable. The rate reductions provided a large windfall gain for high-income persons, in particular owners of old capital. It seems to me relatively difficult to justify such a huge windfall for people owning existing capital.

Both the evolutionary system and the 1986 system would improve static allocative efficiency. The 1986 act is virtually certain to have gone further toward neutrality among business investments than a series of base-broadening bills would have. Since the two alternatives raise the effective tax rate on business capital, they worsen the bias against business assets and in favor of owner-occupied housing. On balance, I suspect that the static allocative efficiency of the 1986 act is better than that of a series of base-broadening tax increases.

As for the impact on saving and growth, either alternative reduces incentives to invest and save. It is unlikely that the series of base-broadening changes would include repeal of IRAs. That is too direct a tax increase on voters to be part of such a policy. Nor, however, would it

37

include tax rate reductions, which increase the incentive to save. On balance, I do not know which system would encourage private saving most. More important, I think that is not the key issue with respect to national saving and economic growth.

Given the developments of the 1980s, the key to growth and national saving is the revenue sufficiency of the system. Here an advantage of the 1986 act, its stability, is its greatest disadvantage. The 1986 act makes it extremely difficult to raise large amounts of additional revenues. It is politically nearly impossible to enact income tax increases on the order of those in 1982 and 1984, given the post-1986 tax system. An alternative system that would have used base-broadening to raise revenues would serve the interest of promoting saving and growth much more than the 1986 act did.

The stability of our current tax system is likely to prevent enactment of new tax preferences for saving, much as it will prevent significant revenue increases. Given our very low levels of private and, more important, national saving, I do not doubt that many will call for saving incentives—including, for example, a return to IRAs. This is not a new phenomenon; throughout the 1970s and 1981 many identified some particular economic need and called for tax preferences to encourage meeting that need.

This could have led to many tax preferences from 1970 to 1981, because bracket creep provided a fiscal dividend. Bracket creep is gone and the fiscal dividend is only a memory, however, while the 1986 act politically forestalls acceptable income tax increases. Huge fiscal deficits will prevent a return to the days of proliferating tax preferences. The result will be a rather stable tax system with a generally sound structure, but one that is woefully inadequate for the financing needs of the federal government.

6

The Effects of Public Policy on Private Saving

Rudolph G. Penner

What follows is, first, some background information on the recent history of U.S. saving as portrayed by official statistics, and second, an examination of the effects of the growing social security trust fund and selected spending programs on national saving. It is conceivable that specific spending programs are more important to private saving decisions than are the tax policy decisions that so often form the focus of the public policy debate. This essay ends with a discussion of the effects of the new budget process on the political feasibility of policies aimed at reducing disincentives to saving.

The Official Record

The official data on saving are flawed in many respects and require adjustment. The chapter by Robert Eisner will suggest a number of adjustments that make the saving problem appear less serious than portrayed by the official data, but in my view the adjustments do not make the problem go away altogether. It is therefore useful to begin with a look at the official numbers. Figure 6–1 shows that for the period 1970–1982, gross national savings were sufficient to finance gross investment and there was no apparent trend in either time series. After 1982, however, national savings began to fall short of investment. Investment maintained its share of GNP with the help of a net inflow of foreign capital, but foreign-financed investment adds less to the national welfare than domestically financed investment because of the addition to the after-tax interest and dividends that must be transferred abroad.

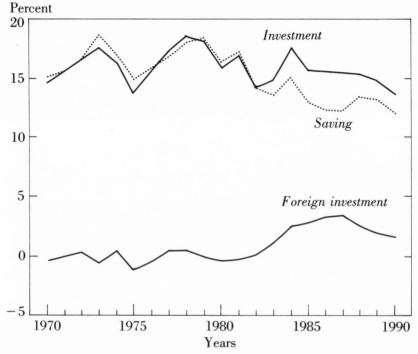

SOURCE: Author.

Figures 6–2 and 6–3 identify the sources of the savings shortfall. Business saving and the saving of state and local government have held up well as a share of GNP. It is the decline in personal saving and the federal deficit that have pulled the saving rate downward.

Figure 6–4 examines the recent history of net saving: that is, of gross saving after deducting depreciation. If depreciation is measured properly, net saving gives us a better idea of the rate at which we are adding to national wealth. Both net national saving and net private saving, here defined to include the surpluses of state and local government, have been on a pronounced downward trend since the early 1970s. The difference between net private and net national saving, as here defined, is the federal deficit. Figure 6–4 clearly illustrates its important role in reducing the rate at which we are accumulating assets. As chapter 14 points out, this statement ignores the possible effect of the deficit as a stimulus to economic activity, and different economists view

40

FIGURE 6–2

GROSS BUSINESS SAVING AND PERSONAL
SAVING AS A PERCENTAGE OF GNP, 1970–1990

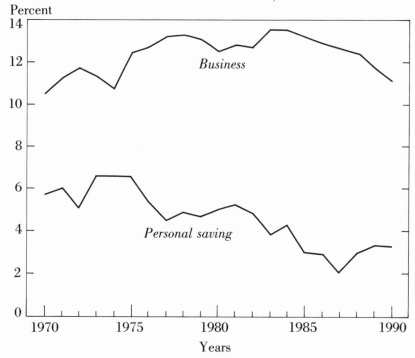

SOURCE: Author.

the importance of this effect very differently. In my view, much of the deficit stimulus of the early 1980s was drained off abroad.[1] To the extent that any fiscal stimulus remained, I suspect that monetary policy could have been looser in its absence.

In examining saving trends, it is important to note that the level of savings is not all that is important. One must also ask how efficiently the savings have been allocated. The thrift fiasco of the 1980s resulted in a terrible waste of the nation's scarce savings during the decade. The tax incentives for investment in the early 1980s also inadvertently created a number of inefficiencies, a problem that was attacked in the Tax Reform Act of 1986. There is still a major difference between the tax treatment of business investment and owner-occupied homes, however, and the efficiency of the total allocation of the nation's capital stock may not have been improved.

41

FIGURE 6–3
FEDERAL, STATE, AND LOCAL GOVERNMENT
SAVING AS A PERCENTAGE OF GNP, 1970–1990

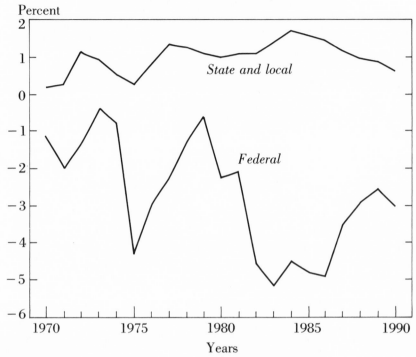

SOURCE: Author.

Social Insurance and Private Saving

Although almost any spending program has the potential to affect the saving rate to some degree, most analysts focus on social insurance programs, especially social security, as being the most likely to have a substantial effect. Certainly nonwelfare social insurance programs are of enormous quantitative importance, accounting for about 35 percent of total spending and more than half of nondefense, noninterest spending. Their impact on saving is crucially dependent on what they are substitutes for. If they are substitutes for private precautionary and pension saving, they are likely to imply an enormous reduction in total national saving. If they are substitutes for intrafamily and other private transfers, one can think of government social insurance programs as a socialization of transfers that would occur in any case, and the effect on the saving rate may be minimal.

The issue has been joined most vigorously in the Martin Feldstein–

42

FIGURE 6–4
NET PRIVATE AND NET NATIONAL
SAVING AS A PERCENTAGE OF GNP, 1970–1990

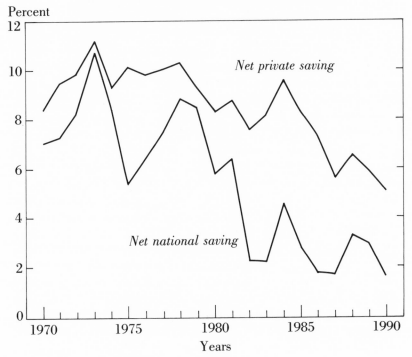

NOTE: Private saving includes state and local surpluses. The difference between the two lines is the federal deficit.

SOURCE: Author.

Robert Barro debate over the effects of social security.[2] Feldstein, seeing social security primarily as a substitute for private pensions, believes that the negative effect on private saving is very large. Barro, seeing social security primarily as a substitute for transfers from children to parents, thinks that the effect on saving is negligible. Both present empirical evidence supporting their cases, and other empirical studies have not firmly supported one side or the other.

I have been looking into the question as to how the elderly lived before social security.[3] My preconceived notion was that they were largely supported by their children. While such support was important, I have been surprised by the variety of support systems that existed in the nineteenth and early twentieth centuries. Unions, fraternal organi-

43

zations, local governments, charities, and numerous other nonfederal collective entities provided substantial social insurance, and at the turn of the century corporate pension programs were growing rapidly—a movement that was subsequently curbed by the Great Depression.

Unfortunately there is no comprehensive quantitative evidence to indicate the relative importance of different means of support, nor to determine the extent to which such support was financed by investments or by pay-as-you-go mechanisms. I suspect, however, that the latter approach predominated and that social security is largely a substitute for traditional private pay-as-you-go transfers. That alone would suggest that the current system has little effect on national saving, but the traditional system was not nearly as generous as social security relative to living standards. I would speculate that some portion of social security is today a substitute for private pensions. Indeed, many private pension systems are integrated with social security in a way that ensures that increases in the payroll tax base automatically reduce private pension contributions. It is my conclusion, therefore, that there are elements of truth in both the Feldstein and the Barro approaches to the problem; although the Feldstein analysis greatly exaggerates the quantitative impact of social security on saving, there is still plenty of room for a significant negative impact. Changes in the social security system, such as the increase in the normal retirement age that was enacted in 1983, may have a more significant impact on the saving rate than some of the super IRAs and other policy changes that are the focus of this conference.

Trust Fund Surpluses and Federal Government Saving

Feldstein and Barro carried out their debate at a time when the social security system was clearly financed according to a pay-as-you-go philosophy. Today, both the social security and the hospital insurance trust funds are running significant surpluses. It is important to ask what that does to the federal budget deficit: that is, to federal dissaving. Many who supported moving the social security system off budget believed that the surplus in the trust funds was simply being spent by the rest of the government—that the trust fund surpluses had no effect on national saving. They believed that if greater attention were drawn to the rest of the government's deficit, more vigorous attempts would be made to reduce it.[4] That proposition has yet to be tested, but it can be noted that despite the accounting change implemented last fall, the press and the

OMB and the Congressional Budget Office (CBO) still focus on the total unified deficit.

I question whether the existence of trust fund surpluses is in fact indirectly raising the deficit, dollar for dollar, in the rest of government. The fiscal policy mistakes that led to the current deficit were made long before the trust funds were in surplus. Immediately after making the mistakes, the Congress began to correct them. The question is whether the speed of the correction was as rapid as could be tolerated by the political system, or whether the political constraints could have been broken if the deficit had appeared to be even more serious. I doubt that the constraints would have been broken. They may have been moved a little in the absence of the trust fund surpluses, but I suspect that the propensity to spend out of those surpluses is considerably less than one.

The Budget Process and the Evaluation of Policies

My last topic involves the effect of the budget process on the evaluation of policies that would reduce saving disincentives. It is often alleged that the budget process is biased against such policies in two ways. First, the revenue implications of such policies should be judged over the very long run, but the budget process arbitrarily requires that policies be deficit-neutral in the first year and over a five-year period. Second, the revenue estimates associated with such policies are done on a static basis, assuming that saving behavior is not affected, and therefore no consideration is given to a possible feedback effect on the rate of economic growth and on revenues in the long run.

In judging these issues, one is faced with a practical dilemma. In the economist's ideal world, all spending and tax policies would be evaluated over the long run and traded off against each other so that long-run marginal social costs and benefits would be equalized. But such a process would involve millions of individual policy decisions each year, and there is not time for that. Budgeting, both in the Congress and in the executive branch, often involves the application of rules of thumb to economize on the time and information required to make decisions. Consequently we observe the application of rules that make little sense to an economist, such as equal across-the-board spending cuts or the stipulation of an arbitrary single-year deficit target.

Prior to Gramm-Rudman such rules could be applied with considerable flexibility. If the application of a rule led to an obviously irrational result an exception could be made—if not in the same budget year, then in the next one. If legislators were able to convince their colleagues that

45

a particular policy would have very beneficial behavioral results in the long run then the policy could be enacted, even if estimators at the joint committee or the CBO did not feel able to estimate that result with precision, and even if the enactment of the policy meant that an officially estimated deficit target could not be reached in the short run.

Gramm-Rudman can be thought of as a law that put an enormous number of rules of thumb into legislative concrete. Those particular rules were so irrational as to be unworkable, but the new process that replaced Gramm-Rudman modified the rules so that they are at least workable and somewhat less irrational.

The Congress chose to tie its own hands, because it worried about what its hands would do if they were free. My description of the pre–Gramm-Rudman world makes it seem as though exceptions to various rules of thumb were rational, but it must also be admitted that exceptions were often fiscally irresponsible.

A part of me strongly believes that, at this moment in history, some sort of arbitrary constraints are necessary to discipline the system. Another part of me deplores the impact of those arbitrary constraints. I deplore the power that the new process gives to official estimators in the bureaucracy. Estimates and arcane scoring decisions made by unelected officials often determine whether a policy option can or cannot be considered. Just as important, regardless of how the estimates are made, the pay-as-you-go rules prevent the consideration of a whole array of policy options that might cost money for certain periods, but could be extremely beneficial in the longer run. They also alter the microeconomics of decision making. For example, they provide an advantage to savings policies that exempt the return to capital from taxation as opposed to allowing a deduction for IRA contributions, because the latter would have a larger immediate effect on the deficit. Even better are policies that provide an initial revenue windfall, although they may be quite irrational in the long run.

But as with any policy, the new budget process has to be judged according to its benefits and costs. It has disciplined the system very effectively this year, and if it continues to work well in the next fiscal year its contribution to national saving by restraining the deficit will far exceed the effects of any policies that it might outlaw. Moreover, its very rigidity implies that it will have to be renegotiated soon. At that time, room can be made for policies that violate the current rules. Put another way, the new system may imply that we have to wait a bit longer for obvious irrationalities caused by rules of thumb to be corrected, but only a very little bit longer than under the pre–Gramm-Rudman system.

If we are really concerned about the very long run, the difference is not very important.

Nevertheless, I yearn for the day that we can escape budgeting that uses legislated rules that are stultifying in their complexity and capricious in their effects. It is too bad that common sense budgeting cannot be legislated. That is what we need and it should be our goal for the long run. Unfortunately, the long run is looking longer every day.

PART THREE

The Experience of Marginal Tax Incentives and Personal Saving under IRAs

7

Past Experience and Current Proposals for IRAs

Larry J. Ozanne

The decline in the personal saving rate in the 1980s has rekindled interest in tax incentives for savings. Many in Congress have endorsed an expansion of individual retirement accounts (IRAs) to additional workers and to preretirement uses. President George Bush has also proposed a tax-favored savings account primarily for preretirement uses. To help assess the effectiveness of these proposals, I examine the savings effect of IRAs between 1982 and 1986. In addition, I compare the incentives of the front-loaded IRA used in that period with the incentives of the back-loaded IRA, which is also being considered today.

Background

IRAs were first allowed by the Employee Retirement Income Security Act of 1974. These IRAs were restricted to employees who were not covered by an employer pension. Their purpose was to extend to workers without pensions the same tax advantages granted through employer pensions to covered employees and to the self-employed. In accordance with the taxation of qualified plans, the 1974 act allowed employees without pensions to deduct contributions to IRAs and to accrue investment earnings without paying tax. Instead, withdrawals from the accounts were included in taxable income. To direct the use of these accounts toward retirement saving, an additional tax of 10 percent was added to withdrawals before age fifty-nine and a half.[1]

IRA eligibility was extended to all persons with earnings by the Economic Recovery Tax Act of 1981. In addition to expanding eligibility

51

as of 1982, the act raised the contribution limit per account from the lesser of 15 percent of earnings or $1,500, to 100 percent of earnings or $2,000.

IRA eligibility was curtailed in the Tax Reform Act of 1986, but the restrictions differed from those of the 1974 act. Starting in 1987, contributions to IRAs were not deductible for persons or couples with pension coverage and with incomes above certain limits. The income limits were $35,000 for unmarried taxpayers and $50,000 for married taxpayers filing a joint return. The contribution limits were phased out beginning at income levels $10,000 below the cutoffs. In addition, couples were treated as a unit for determining pension coverage. If either spouse was covered through employment, both were subject to the restrictions on deductible contributions. Finally, nondeductible contributions were allowed to the extent deductible contributions were disallowed.

The expansion of IRA eligibility in 1982 led to a surge in the number of persons contributing to IRAs and the total amount they contributed. Curtailment of eligibility in 1987 reduced this surge. In 1981, 3 million tax filers deducted a total of $5 billion in IRA contributions. IRA contributors and contributions jumped in 1982 and reached a peak in 1985. In that year 16 million tax filers deducted $39 billion in IRA contributions. IRA used dropped precipitously in 1987—just 7 million tax filers deducted $14 billion in contributions (table 7–1).

TABLE 7–1

IRA CONTRIBUTORS AND CONTRIBUTIONS, 1981–1987

Year	Tax Returns with IRA Contribution (millions)	Dollars Contributed (billions)
1981	3	5
1982	12	28
1983	14	32
1984	15	35
1985	16	39
1986	16	38
1987	7	14

SOURCE: Internal Revenue Service.

LARRY J. OZANNE

Were IRA Contributions Increased Savings?

Whether the large flow of funds into IRAs between 1982 and 1986 increased personal saving depends on what the contributors would have done with those funds in the absence of IRAs. If in the absence of IRAs they would have primarily gone out to eat more often, purchased more luxurious automobiles, and otherwise consumed more, then contributing instead to IRAs primarily increased saving. Conversely, if they would have primarily run up larger balances in other savings accounts, or paid off their mortgage and other debts faster, then contributing to IRAs mostly did not increase saving. In the latter case, contributing to an IRA primarily diverted savings into new accounts.

To answer the question of whether the expansion of IRAs increased saving, therefore, it is necessary to infer what contributors would have done with their contributions in the absence of IRAs. I will draw inferences about behavior in the absence of IRAs from descriptions of those who contributed to IRAs. Others have drawn inferences from formal modeling and econometric estimation of the savings decision.[2]

Who Contributed to IRAs?

IRA contributors were a select group. Even though all persons with compensation were eligible to contribute to IRAs between 1982 and 1986, most did not do so regularly. In 1985, the year of peak IRA use, only 18 percent of tax returns with earnings reported IRA contributions.[3]

The select group who contributed to IRAs mostly contributed the legal maximum. For individual taxpayers, the maximum was $2,000. For couples with only one paid worker and filing jointly, the maximum was $2,250. For couples with two paid workers, the maximum was $2,000 each, or $4,000 per joint return. Few people who contributed to IRAs were restrained from contributing up to these maximums because their earnings were less than these maximums.

In 1985, 61 percent of tax returns that reported IRA contributions reported contributions at the legal maximum. In addition, many joint returns reported contributions of exactly $2,000 even though the couples were eligible for contributions of $2,250 or $4,000. The contribution of exactly $2,000 suggests that one spouse contributed the maximum while the other spouse contributed nothing. If these joint returns are counted as maximum contributions, the percentage of tax returns with a maximum contribution rises from 61 percent to 77 percent.

Most contributors had sizable amounts of other assets that could easily be transferred to IRAs; few noncontributors did. Based on reported amounts of dividends and taxable interest income, an estimated 63 percent of contributors in 1985 had more than $10,000 in savings accounts, taxable bonds, and stocks. Only 13 percent of noncontributors had that much.

Contributors also tended to be older workers. Using family surveys, William G. Gale and John Karl Scholz found that 21 percent of IRA contributors between 1983 and 1986 were age fifty-nine or older.[4] Those over fifty-nine and a half could withdraw contributions at any time without penalty. Using a separate survey, Steven F. Venti and David A. Wise showed that IRA participation in 1984 increased strongly with age, as shown in table 7–2.

IRA contributors also were likely to be covered by an employer pension, have some college education, and be married. In 1983, 70 percent of workers with an IRA also participated in a pension.[5] In the same year, the probability of contributing to an IRA was significantly higher among households in which the head or the head's spouse had more than twelve years of formal education.[6] Finally, 72 percent of tax returns reporting IRA contributions in 1985 were joint returns.

From these characteristics of IRA contributors emerges the profile of typical IRA contributors. The typical IRA contributors were middle-aged, college-educated couples who were covered by an employer pension plan and had substantial amounts of other financial assets.

TABLE 7–2

IRA PARTICIPATION BY AGE, 1984

Age of Head of Household	Families with IRA Contributions (%)
Under 25	2.4
25–34	10.9
35–44	22.2
45–54	29.4
55–64	34.9

SOURCE: Steven F. Venti and David A. Wise, "The Saving Effect of Tax Deferred Retirement Accounts: Evidence from SIPP," in B. Douglas Bernheim and John B. Shoven, eds., *National Saving and Economic Performance* (Chicago: University of Chicago Press, 1991), p. 108, table 4.2B.

Did IRAs Cause the Typical Contributors to Save More?

There are good reasons to expect that the typical contributors primarily diverted other savings to IRAs rather than saved more. The possibility that typical contributors primarily increased their saving, however, cannot be ruled out. I examine both views.

Reasons for Diverting Savings. The typical contributors had enough financial assets in other accounts that they could contribute up to the IRA maximum without any increase in savings. Furthermore, they probably would have been adding to these other accounts with new savings even in the absence of IRAs, and these new savings could be redirected to IRAs. Why, then, should the typical contributors have funded their IRAs by eating out less often or buying a less luxurious car? They could have obtained the full tax benefits of IRAs simply by diverting other savings into IRAs.

Because the typical contributors could have filled their accounts up to the legal maximum by diverting other savings, they appear to have had no marginal incentive to increase their saving rate. In this situation, IRAs only provide a reduction in taxes, and persons who find their taxes reduced are likely to consume more instead of save more. [7]

The large fraction of persons reported above to be contributing the maximum is consistent with the view that typical contributors were diverting assets. People with substantial amounts of existing assets available to transfer to IRAs and with continual savings to redirect to IRAs would contribute the maximum each year at least until they ran out of other savings to transfer and to redirect.

The minority of contributors whose contributions were less than the maximum did have a marginal incentive to save more in their IRA. They may not, however, have responded much to this incentive. Empirical studies have not been able to find evidence consistently that Americans increase their saving in response to higher rates of return, which is what IRAs essentially provide.

Higher rates of return provide offsetting influences on the desire to save. The higher return encourages people to save more because another dollar saved buys more than it otherwise would. Conversely, the same amount of future consumption can be achieved by saving less. If these influences largely offset each other for most Americans, even persons contributing less than the maximum to IRAs may not have increased their saving.

In sum, the typical contributors could easily have collected the full tax benefit from IRAs without saving more. Thus they might have had no incentive to save more. Even the minority who contributed less than the maximum, and therefore clearly had an incentive to save more, may not have responded.

Reasons for Increased Saving. Although the typical contributors had other savings that could be diverted to IRAs, they might not have wanted to do so. If that savings were for a down payment on a home, for their children's college education, or for possible emergencies, they might not want it locked up until age fifty-nine and a half. If the typical contributors did not have much savings for retirement, then IRAs would have provided them an incentive to increase their total saving.

Futhermore, the typical IRA contributors may have been responsive to the IRA incentive even though most Americans might not respond to a simple change in the rate of return. IRAs were heavily advertised and offered an upfront deduction. The typical contributors were old enough to become interested in retirement saving and probably were more responsive to savings incentives than the population at large. This combination may have been enough to induce most contributors to increase their saving enough to reach the legal maximum. Finally, the penalty on withdrawals before age fifty-nine and a half may have helped the typical contributors resist spending the funds once they were contributed. In sum, the typical contributors may not have had retirement savings available to transfer into an IRA and may have found the IRA such a good opportunity that they increased their retirement saving up to the legal limit.

Evaluation. Neither interpretation of how the typical contributors funded their IRAs has been proven. In other words, the extent to which IRAs were funded by diverting other savings or by saving more has not been settled.

The arguments for saving much more, however, are less convincing when applied to the typical contributors between 1982 and 1986. First, being middle-aged, the typical contributors probably had considered holding at least some of their assets until age sixty.[8] Thus some assets were probably available for transfer. In addition, the typical contributors might well have been saving enough for retirement each year in the absence of IRAs so that they could continue to fill up their IRA for additional years without having to increase their saving.

Much of the evidence supporting the argument that IRAs increased saving comes from econometric studies that find IRAs increased saving right from the start.[9] Yet the likelihood that the typical contributors had retirement savings to divert to IRAs raises doubts about the conclusions of these studies.

Furthermore, even if advertising and the upfront deduction did convince the typical contributors to use IRAs, they could use them by transferring assets rather than by saving more. Nor would the penalty appear to be necessary for the typical contributors to keep from spending their savings. They had already managed to accumulate substantial amounts of other assets, which they could spend without incurring any tax. Finally, many contributors were either already over age fifty-nine and a half or close enough to it that the penalty was not much of a hurdle.

Implications for Current Legislation

Several proposals for tax-favored savings incentives are before Congress. Two of the most widely discussed are President Bush's proposal for family savings accounts and Senator Lloyd Bentsen and Senator William Roth's bill to expand IRAs. In his 1993 budget, President Bush changed the name of his proposed savings accounts to flexible individual retirement accounts.

In his 1991, 1992, and 1993 budgets, President Bush proposed the creation of special savings accounts that would not be taxed on their investment earnings so long as amounts withdrawn were on deposit for at least seven years. No restrictions would be placed on uses of the withdrawals. Individuals with incomes below $60,000 and couples with incomes below $120,000 would be eligible to contribute up to $2,500 per person to these family savings accounts.

Senators Bentsen and Roth's bill, S. 612, would extend eligibility for the existing IRA deduction to all workers and waive the penalty on withdrawals before age fifty-nine and a half for withdrawals used to purchase a first home, to pay for college education, or to cover medical emergencies. In addition, S. 612 would create a second option resembling the administration's family savings account. The tax benefit would be tax-free investment earnings, withdrawals would be allowed without penalty after five years, and no restrictions would be placed on the use of these withdrawals.

The experience with IRAs suggests that an extension of tax incentives to preretirement uses is likely to result in extensive diversion of savings into the tax-favored accounts. The extension of existing IRAs to all workers, however, should have much less impact than it did in 1982.

Extension of Incentive to Preretirement Uses. Between 1982 and 1986, the typical IRA contributors had substantial assets outside of their IRAs. While we are uncertain whether the typical contributors were diverting these assets into IRAs, we can expect that they would divert savings into tax-favored accounts allowing withdrawals after five to seven years or for common needs like purchasing a home and paying for college. Furthermore, people who did not contribute to IRAs becasue they were saving for preretirement purposes, such as a home or the education of their children, would also divert savings into the tax-favored accounts. Thus, allowing savings for preretirement purposes to be deposited in tax-favored accounts would likely result in the diversion of substantial savings to these accounts.

While substantial diversion of savings is likely, a substantial increase in saving is less likely. As noted, studies of saving have not consistently found that Americans increase their saving much in response to increases in the rate of return. People who were saving for a particular purpose such as college tuition may even save less in response to the incentives because their deposits accumulate faster. Unless the tax reductions from using the accounts are offset by other taxes, the savings incentives could reduce rather than increase saving. Finally, as the uncertainty surrounding IRAs indicates, the effect of the incentives on saving is likely to be in doubt even if they are widely used.[10]

Extending IRAs to All Workers. A simple extension of traditional IRAs to currently ineligible employees would probably cause a much smaller increase in IRA contributions than did the 1982 extension of IRA eligibilty. The main reason is that many more employees now have access to saving plans like IRAs through their employer than did so in 1982. The impact would also be less than in 1982 because lower-income employees with pensions are already eligible for these IRAs, because others are already eligible for nondeductible IRAs, and because tax rates are lower now.

Most employers now are allowed to offer salary reduction savings plans to their employees under extensions of the laws allowing employer pension plans. For-profit employers can offer salary reduction through Section 401(k) of the Internal Revenue Code, educational and certain other nonprofit employers can offer salary reduction through Section 403(b), state and local governments can offer salary reduction through Section 457, and the federal government offers salary reduction through its thrift savings plan.

Salary reduction plans receive the same tax treatment as IRAs. In

58

these plans, the amount employees elect to contribute to a retirement savings account is excluded from taxable income. Earnings of the account accumulate tax-free. Withdrawals are included in taxable income, and withdrawals before age fifty-nine and a half are subject to an extra tax of 10 percent.

Salary reduction plans have other advantages that IRAs do not. Contributions can be in excess of $2,000; employers often supplement contributions with matching contributions; many employers allow preretirement borrowing against the contributions; and retirement annuities can usually be purchased through the plan at the lower rates available to group purchases.

Salary reduction plans were not widely used in 1982 when IRAs were first extended to all workers. Section 401(k) was added in the Revenue Act of 1978, but regulations for implementing salary reduction plans under this section were not issued until 1981. In 1982 fewer than 2 million workers contributed to salary reduction plans. These plans have spread since, and by 1990, 41 percent of employees in medium and large firms and one-sixth of employees in small firms had access to 401(k) plans. When salary reduction plans for nonprofit institutions and governments are included, the total number of families in which someone contributes to a salary reduction plan today is probably similar to the number with IRA contributions in 1985, the peak year of IRA use.

Because salary reduction plans are widespread today, fewer workers today than in 1982 have retirement savings in taxable accounts that could be diverted to IRAs. In fact, most employees with salary reduction plans are not contributing up to the maximum allowed in those plans and would be unlikely to contribute at all to IRAs. Thus extending IRAs to all workers today would be largely equivalent to extending salary reduction opportunities to upper-income families in which at least one worker has a pension but neither worker has an employer-based salary reduction plan. The number of people in such situations who would use IRAs is undoubtedly much smaller than the number who took up IRAs in the early 1980s.

What Do Front-Loaded and Back-Loaded IRAs Offer?

The IRA in use since 1974 has become known as a front-loaded IRA to distinguish it from the recently proposed accounts that allow no upfront deduction but do not tax withdrawals. These accounts, such as the administration's family savings account and the alternative savings option in S. 612, are referred to as back-loaded IRAs.

Referring to the newly proposed savings accounts as back-loaded IRAs is convenient but not entirely accurate. First, the IRA part suggests retirement saving, but neither proposal is restricted to retirement saving. Withdrawals for any purpose are allowed without penalty after five years from the S. 612 option and after seven years from family savings accounts. Second, the tax benefits are not back-loaded. Withdrawals from normal savings accounts are not taxed. Therefore tax-free withdrawals from these accounts is no benefit. The tax benefit comes from not taxing the investment earnings of the account, and this benefit accrues throughout the time the funds are on deposit. These distinctions should be kept in mind when the term "back-loaded IRA" is applied to the recent proposals.

In addition, front- and back-loaded IRAs can actually be similar in ways they look different, and they can be different in ways they look the same. Front- and back-loaded IRAs, for example, appear to offer different savings incentives, but their incentives turn out to be equivalent in common circumstances. Futhermore, when both types of IRAs appear to allow the same maximum contribution limit, for example, $2,000 as in S. 612, the back-loaded IRA actually allows a higher effective contribution.

Comparing Saving Incentives. The tax benefit from a front-loaded IRA is the same as from a back-loaded IRA when a person faces the same marginal tax rate at the time of withdrawal as at the time of contribution. In this case the tax paid on the front-loaded IRA at withdrawal is equal to the tax avoided on the contribution plus interest for the delay in payment. The remaining advantage is tax-free interest on the aftertax amount of the contribution. Since the back-loaded IRA is an aftertax contribution with tax-free interest, the benefits of the front- and back-loaded IRAs are equivalent in this case.

The example in table 7–3 illustrates this equivalence of the tax incentives when tax rates are the same at the time of deposit and withdrawal. Consider a fifty-year-old man who decides to devote $1,000 of his pretax wages to saving for retirement ten years later. He is in the 28 percent tax bracket throughout the ten years and earns 8 percent interest on all savings. Without an IRA this man would have $280 of taxes withheld from his $1,000 of wages, leaving him $720 to deposit in a passbook savings account. Although the deposit would earn 8 percent, he would withdraw 28 percent of each year's interest to pay the tax due. After ten years the account would accumulate to $1,261. As no further taxes would be due, the full amount would be available for spending.

60

TABLE 7–3
BENEFITS FROM FRONT- AND BACK-LOADED IRAs WITH EQUAL TAX
RATES AT DEPOSIT AND WITHDRAWAL

	Passbook Account	Type of IRA	
		Back	Front
Wages ($)	1,000	1,000	1,000
Tax rate on wages (%)	28	28	0
Deposit ($)	720	720	1,000
Interest rate (%)	8	8	8
Tax rate on interest (%)	28	0	0
Years until withdrawal	10	10	10
Amount withdrawn ($)	1,261	1,554	2,159
Tax rate on withdrawal (%)	0	0	28
Amount available for spending ($)	1,261	1,554	1,554

SOURCE: Author.

If the man instead had access to a back-loaded IRA, he would not have to withdraw 28 percent of his interest earnings each year to pay tax. After ten years of earning tax-free interest, the account would have grown to $1,554. As with the passbook account, the full balance would be available for spending.

If the man had access to a front-loaded IRA, he would be able to deposit the full $1,000 in the account because the deduction exempts that portion of wages from tax. After earning 8 percent interest for ten years, the account would have built up to $2,159. The withdrawal, however, would be taxed at a 28 percent rate, leaving $1,554 available for spending. This amount is the same as in the back-loaded example. Thus when tax rates are the same at the time of deposit and withdrawal, the front-loaded IRA provides the same tax benefit as a back-loaded IRA. Both offer tax-free interest on the aftertax value of the deposit.

People need not be in the same tax bracket when they withdraw funds from their IRA as they were when they contributed to it. If the tax rate at withdrawal is lower, they get an additional tax break in a front-loaded IRA because they shift the recognition of income to a year with a lower tax rate. This most commonly occurs when people withdraw funds in retirement. If the man described in table 7–3, for example, had fallen into the 15 percent tax bracket when he retired at age sixty, he would have been able to keep $1,835 from his front-loaded IRA. The return from the back-loaded IRA and the passbook account would be unaffected by this change.

Conversely, if the tax rate at withdrawal is higher than when the contribution was made, then the benefit from a front-loaded IRA is reduced. The disadvantage from paying a higher tax at withdrawal can be so large that the person keeps less aftertax than if the funds had been placed in a fully taxed savings account. A modification of the above example illustrates this point. Suppose that the man in the above example had been twenty-five years old, in the 15 percent tax bracket, and saving for a down payment on a home. Just before withdrawal at age thirty-five, however, his income increases enough to edge him into the 28 percent tax bracket. As table 7–4 shows, he would have the least to put down on a home from a front-loaded IRA (even if no penalty tax were due at that age). From a front-loaded IRA he would have $1,554, from a normally taxed passbook account he would have $1,641, and from a back-loaded IRA he would have $1,835.[11]

The lowering of the tax advantage from being in a higher tax bracket at the time of withdrawal would be most likely to occur for younger people saving for preretirement purposes, such as a down payment on a home, for a car, or for their children's educational needs. Thus a back-

TABLE 7–4

BENEFITS FROM FRONT- AND BACK-LOADED IRAs WITH HIGHER TAX RATE AT WITHDRAWAL THAN AT DEPOSIT

	Passbook Account	Type of IRA	
		Back	Front
Wages ($)	1,000	1,000	1,000
Tax rate on wages (%)	15	15	0
Deposit ($)	850	850	1,000
Interest rate (%)	8	8	8
Tax rate on interest (%)	15	0	0
Years until withdrawal	10	10	10
Amount withdrawn ($)	1,641	1,835	2,159
Tax rate on withdrawal (%)	0	0	28
Amount available for spending ($)	1,641	1,835	1,554

SOURCE: Author.

loaded IRA, which offers only tax-free interest, may be better suited than a front-loaded IRA for a preretirement savings incentive.

Comparing Contribution Limits. When front- and back-loaded IRAs have the same dollar contribution limit, they provide unequal tax benefits. In this case the back-loaded IRA offers the greater benefit. As the example in table 7–3 shows, a contribution of $720 to a back-loaded IRA provides the same amount of spending after withdrawal as does a contribution of $1,000 to a front-loaded IRA. If the back-loaded IRA had been allowed the same $1,000 deposit as the front-loaded IRA, it would have provided greater benefit. The back-loaded IRA provides greater benefit per dollar of contribution because no further tax is due on that contribution. In contrast, a portion of the contribution to the front-loaded IRA will be taken in taxes at withdrawal.

8

IRAs and Saving

David A. Wise

Over the past several years I have written a series of papers with Steven Venti on the saving effect of individual retirement accounts (IRAs). This chapter has been abstracted from our paper on "Government Policy and Personal Retirement Saving."[1]

Our analysis has been based on three data sets: the Consumer Expenditure Surveys (CES), the Survey of Consumer Finances (SCF), and most recently, the Survey of Income and Program Participation (SIPP).[1] The evidence suggests that the bulk of IRA contributions represents net new saving; that is, we are unable to find much substitution of IRA for non-IRA financial assets. Much of our previous analysis is based on formal and somewhat complex econometric models.

In this chapter I present the basic patterns of IRA and non-IRA saving behavior, without the constraints imposed by the more formal models. The descriptive data are, however, consistent with our formal model estimates. The data that I will discuss in this chapter represent the basic facts with which any formal model must contend. I will then comment on the strategy that we followed in the more formal analysis.

Background

On the eve of retirement the typical American family has only about $6,600 in financial assets, according to the SIPP. The decline in the aggregate personal saving rate in the United States over the past few decades is well known. The typical American family has about $1,500 in financial assets.

The explosion of IRA saving after the 1981 legislation can be judged by comparing assets in IRA accounts with firm pension fund .assets, reflecting the retirement saving by firms for their employees. Assets in IRA and Keogh accounts were only about 4 percent as large as pension fund assets in 1981. By 1989, accumulation of personal saving in IRA accounts amounted to $493.7 billion and was almost 27 percent as large as pension fund assets. Without the precipitous decline in IRA contributions after the 1986 bill, IRA assets would apparently have continued to grow.

IRAs are sometimes portrayed as held by only a few and concentrated among the wealthy. According to SIPP data, families earning less that $50,000 annually held 76 percent of IRA accounts in 1986 and 66 percent of total IRA assets. About one-quarter of all households had accounts in 1986. But a much larger fraction of households with modest lifetime incomes would have been IRA savers under the pre-1986 legislation. The percentage of households with IRA accounts in 1986 ranged from close to zero for young households with very low incomes to more than 70 percent among older households with high incomes.[2]

Like other saving, IRA saving increases with age and income. More than 50 percent of households with annual income above $20,000 would have opened an IRA account before they retired, based on the 1986 participation rate of households with heads fifty-five to sixty-five and income above $20,000. About 60 percent in this age bracket with incomes above $30,000 had accounts, as did 65 percent of those with incomes above $40,000. Relative to other saving, then, IRA saving is very widespread. In particular, IRAs may be accurately portrayed as widespread among potential savers.

IRA Saving versus Other Saving, 1980–1989

If IRA saving substituted for other saving, one might expect the proportion of persons saving in other forms to decline as the proportion saving through IRAs increased. Figure 8–1 shows the proportion of households contributing to an IRA in each year and the proportion of households with positive saving in non-IRA assets. The data in figure 8–1 include stocks and bonds. A comparable figure that excludes stocks and bonds is shown in Venti and Wise. Throughout this chapter data will typically be shown excluding stocks and bonds. Comparable data that include stocks and bonds reveal the same patterns and are reported in Venti and Wise.[3] Figure 8–1 shows that between 1980 and 1989 there was essentially no change in the proportion of households with non-IRA financial asset saving. The proportion making IRA contributions grew

FIGURE 8–1

IRA VERSUS NON-IRA SAVING,

INCLUDING STOCKS AND BONDS, 1980–1989

(proportion of households with positive saving)

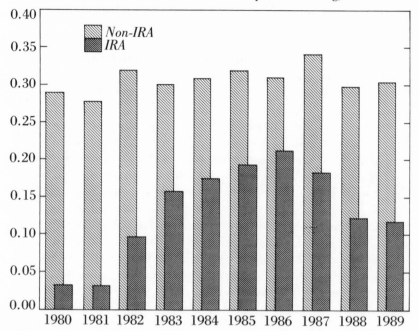

from 3 percent to 20 percent and then declined to 10 percent after the 1986 legislation.

Although we would expect the proportion of households with other saving to decline if there were widespread substitution of IRAs for other saving, it is possible that even if IRA savers reduced other saving, most would still have some saving in other forms. In this case, the proportion with positive non-IRA saving would not change much. Thus we turn to consideration of the change in saving balances.

Change in IRA versus Non-IRA Balances

This section examines whether the data appear consistent with the possibility that IRA contributions represented no addition to total saving, but rather a reshuffling of existing asset balances or a switching of new saving from non-IRA to IRA accounts. The analysis is based on

66

the changes in non-IRA financial asset balances as IRA balances increased. Do non-IRA balances decline, as the substitution, or reshuffling, hypothesis suggests? Substitution could occur in two ways. Either existing pre-1982 assets were transferred into IRAs in subsequent years or, beginning in 1982, new saving was in the form of IRAs instead of non-IRA financial assets—in other words, IRA saving displaced non-IRA saving.

Two versions of the change in non-IRA balances are discussed. The first is based on the balances of respondents to successive Consumer Expenditure Surveys, but they are adjusted for the change in the attributes of contributor respondents to the surveys. The comparison is based on the balances of the random samples interviewed in successive surveys; the same respondents are not followed from year to year. The second version compares the balances of the same respondents interviewed through the Survey of Consumer Finances in 1983 and 1986. The goal is to judge whether the increase in IRA balances was accompanied by a transfer of assets from non-IRA accounts or by a reduction in new saving in non-IRA assets.

IRA versus Non-IRA Asset Balances, CES Data, 1980 and 1986. Each quarter the Consumer Expenditure Survey obtains information on a new random sample of households. Thus each survey represents a snapshot of households in that quarter. Data are obtained on income, assets, and other household characteristics. The average age of the head of the respondent households was about forty-six in each of the quarterly samples. Combined data from the quarterly surveys yield annual averages. These data are merged with IRA balances obtained from the SIPP, from 1985 to 1987.

These data can be used to compare the pre-1982 assets of persons who were "like" those who made IRA contributions in 1986. That is, we ask for the assets in 1980 of households who were like the households who made IRA contributions in 1986. In 1980 most of the like households were not eligible for an IRA. But by defining like groups, the 1980 and 1986 assets of comparable households can be compared. The groups are comparable except for the 1986 respondents having had the opportunity to make IRA contributions for several years, while the 1980 respondents had not.[4]

I will refer here only to the comparison between 1980 and 1986 shown in table 8–1.[5] The 1980 IRA balance of contributor-like respondent households was close to zero. By 1986 the median had increased to $7,800. Contributor-like 1980 respondents had a median of $4,635

TABLE 8-1
CES-SIPP SUMMARY, EXCLUDING STOCKS AND BONDS, 1980 AND 1986
(dollars)

Contributor Status and Asset	Respondents in		% Change
	1980	1986	
Contributor-like			
Non-IRA assets	4,635	7,816	68.6
IRA assets	0	7,800	—
Total assets	4,635	17,900	286.2
Non-Contributor-like			
Total assets	508	752	48.0

SOURCE: Author's calculations.

in non-IRA financial assets. The 1986 respondents had a median of $7,816 in non-IRA assets, representing an increase of 69 percent. In addition to the increase in non-IRA assets, the 1986 contributors had an additional $7,800 in IRA assets. Total financial assets of contributor-like respondents increased from about $4,635 in 1980 to about $17,900 in 1986, an increase of 286 percent.

Is it likely that without the IRA program the assets of like households would have nearly tripled over this period? There are at least two reasons why non-IRA assets might have increased. One is that nominal income increased and nominal saving might have increased as well. The other is that changes in the rate of return on financial assets may have changed. The increase in median income between 1980 and 1986 was 48 percent, much less than the increase in total financial assets—286 percent. Indeed the income increase was less than the increase in non-IRA financial assets—69.6 percent. Assets may also have increased because of capital gains in the stock market. But the financial assets of most savers are not in stocks. Indeed, the increase in non-IRA assets excluding stocks and bonds was not much greater than the increase when they were included, suggesting that stock market capital gains are not the explanation.

It may be that non-IRA balances should be considered relative to the total increase in financial assets for all respondents. This increase between 1980 and 1986 was 48 percent, much less than the percentage of increase for contributors.

What about the return on commercial bank accounts, where the bulk of most households' financial assets are held? Average time and saving deposit rates in commercial banks in the years preceding 1980, 1982, 1983, and 1986 are shown in table 8–2. The data for 1983 are included in anticipation of the same issue that will be raised with respect to the data in the next section.

The rate of return for the years preceding 1986 was somewhat higher than the rate in the years preceding 1980, but the differences are not large enough to explain the large increase in financial assets. Even the increase in non-IRA financial assets seems large relative to the increase that might have been expected based on 1980 non-IRA assets.

Based on these data, it seems unlikely that IRA replaced non-IRA saving—that there was no gain in net saving. Again, it is apparent from the low 1980 asset balances of contributor-like households—$4,635— that before the advent of IRAs the typical contributor-like household had not been accumulating financial assets at an annual rate close to an IRA contribution, typically $2,000 or $4,000 in 1986. It is also clear that the increase in IRA balances was not funded by withdrawing funds from pre-1982 balances, which were substantially smaller than the $7,800 put into IRA accounts.[6]

IRA versus Non-IRA Balances, SCF Data, 1983 and 1986. The discussion in the previous section is based on the comparison of the asset balances of the different respondents to successive surveys, before and after the general availability of IRAs. In that case, asset balances

TABLE 8–2
RATES OF RETURN ON TIME AND SAVING DEPOSITS IN COMMERCIAL
BANKS, 1974–1986
(percent)

| Ending in | Average over the Preceding | | | |
	Three Years	Four Years	Five Years	Six Years
1980	7.53	7.02	6.72	6.59
1982	10.28	9.58	8.87	8.31
1983	10.07	9.82	9.35	8.80
1986	7.84	7.99	8.48	8.95

SOURCE: Savings Institutions Handbook, U.S. League of Savings Institutions Headquarters, Washington, D.C., 1989.

may have increased between the surveys because of income growth, but age did not change systematically; the average age was about forty-six in each year. An alternative to comparing different household samples in different years is to compare the balances of the same households over time. In this case, asset balances may increase as the households age, and possibly as their incomes grow as well.

Such a comparison can be made using the 1983 and 1986 SCF data. We begin with respondents to the 1986 survey. Only households aged twenty-four to sixty-five are included in the analysis, and households with self-employed members are excluded. Non-IRA and IRA median balances for this group in 1983 and 1986 and the percentage of change in balances between these years are shown in table 8–3, by 1986 IRA contributor status.[7] These figures also include total assets of contributors—including both IRA and non-IRA balances.

Again, the non-IRA assets of contributors did not decline as IRA assets increased between 1983 and 1986; on the contrary, they increased substantially. The median 1983 non-IRA asset balance, excluding stocks and bonds, of households with IRA accounts in 1986 was $6,360. Prior to 1983, this group clearly had not been accumulating assets at the rate of the typical IRA contribution. And clearly the $6,000 increase in IRA balances—from $1,000 in 1983 to $7,000 in 1986—was not funded by transferring funds from the 1983 balance in non-IRA accounts, $6,360.

Without the IRA program, what increase in this 1983 non-IRA

TABLE 8–3

SURVEY OF CONSUMER FINANCES SUMMARY, EXCLUDING STOCKS AND
BONDS, 1983 AND 1986

(dollars)

Contributor Status and Asset	Respondents in		% Change
	1983	1986	
Contributors in 1986			
Non-IRA assets	6,360	9,209	44.8
IRA assets	1,000	7,000	600.0
Total assets	8,900	20,000	125.7
Non-Contributors in 1986			
Total assets	600	900	50.0

SOURCE: Author's calculations.

asset balance would be expected over the next three years? In fact the observed 44.8 percent increase was equivalent to an annual growth rate of more than 13 percent. The increase in all assets combined, including IRAs, was in fact much greater than this. IRA assets also grew, by $6,000. The median of total assets more than doubled, increasing by $11,100, from $8,900 to $20,000.

Without IRA contributions, would the 1983 balance of $6,360 have been expected to increase by almost threefold, to $20,000, by 1986? As discussed in the previous section, the increase in total assets may be determined in part by income growth and the increase in age, and the data could be confounded by differences in economic trends prior to the two dates—differences in rates of return. The increase in non-IRA assets between 1983 and 1986 is apparently not the result of the growth in stock values over this period. The percentage increase in non-IRA assets was about the same when stocks and bonds were excluded as when they were included.

Assets may have been expected to increase with age and income. We have controlled for these effects by predicting 1986 assets based on the distribution of contributor assets by age and income in 1983. Adjusting for the three-year age increase and the income increase between 1983 and 1986, the balance would have been expected to increase by about 25 percent. Including IRA contributions, the actual increase was almost 126 percent. Commercial bank rates in the years preceding 1986 were lower than the rates preceding 1983, as shown in the previous section. The asset growth cannot be explained by unusually high rates of return.

Thus, judging from the SCF data, it seems unlikely that the IRA contributions were simply substituted for saving that would have occurred anyway. That assumption seems implausible based on the information available in 1983. Based on the 1983 balance of $6,360, the 1986 contributors prior to 1983 had not been accustomed to saving nearly as much as they saved over the next three years. Comparison of the SCF with the CES summary tabulation in the previous section shows that the two data sets yield essentially the same implications.

Change in Other Saving with Change in IRA Status

If it is true that non-IRA saving is reduced when IRA saving is increased, then a household that begins to contribute should reduce non-IRA saving. Likewise, a household that stops contributing should increase non-IRA saving. The SIPP panel data allow calculation of the change in non-IRA saving when IRA contributor-status changes. This calculation controls directly for changes in saving behavior across families, since it is based on changes over time for the same families.[8]

Table 8–4 shows that there is a small reduction—$377—in non-IRA bank account financial-asset saving for new contributors, and a small increase—$148.60—for households that stop contributing. But the changes are only a small fraction of the typical IRA contribution— about $2,300.

Estimates incorporating all non-IRA financial assets—bank accounts, bonds, and stocks—are shown in Venti and Wise.[9] These data also reveal that the change in non-IRA saving is much less than the typical IRA contribution. Although these data suggest some substitution, none of the estimates is statistically significant. In particular, the hypothesis that there is no change in non-IRA saving with change in IRA contributor status cannot be rejected.

More Formal Analysis and Limitations of the Theory

Many observers have expressed views on the saving effects of IRAs that are based not on empirical evidence but on simple theoretical reasoning.[10] In some important respects, however, the empirical evidence is inconsistent with the predictions and the assumptions embedded in the theory-based speculations. Although these models may provide some insight into how people should behave in a narrow financial sense, the predictions offer a poor description of how the public actually responded to the IRA program. Indeed, the assumptions are inconsistent with basic facts about IRA contributors and IRA saving. Moreover, the assumptions underlying the speculations virtually preclude any saving effect of IRAs.

TABLE 8–4
CHANGE IN NON-IRA SAVING IN BANK ACCOUNTS WHEN
IRA SAVING CHANGES
(dollars)

	With No 1985 IRA Saving	With 1985 IRA Saving
No 1984 IRA saving	−65	−377
Had 1984 IRA saving	149	−470

SOURCE: Author's calculations are from the Survey of Income and Program Participation.

A more complete model must recognize the broader economic and psychological channels through which an aggressively promoted tax-advantaged saving plan may stimulate saving. Thus having presented the data, I emphasize the limitations of judgments based on restrictive assumptions about saving behavior that are embedded in the simple economic model. It is important to determine from the data which assumptions are most consistent with the saving decisions of real people.

Four assumptions are embedded in the simple theoretical framework that has been used by some to evaluate the saving effects of IRAs. The first is that most IRA contributors were already saving more than the IRA limit prior to the advent of the IRA program. A related assumption is that the typical IRA saver had large accumulated financial asset balances that could easily be transferred to an IRA account. The second assumption is that the program inducement to save operates entirely through the after-tax rate of return. The IRA tax advantage encourages saving by increasing the return on saving, up to the IRA limit. But a household that is already saving more than the limit does not benefit from the higher rate of return on an additional dollar saved. The third and most important assumption is that IRA saving and other forms of saving are treated by savers as perfect substitutes. The fourth, related to the third, is that the promotion of IRA saving had no effect on its use.

It seems apparent from the data presented above that the typical IRA contributor, prior to the advent of the IRA program, had not been saving nearly as much as the typical IRA contribution—about $2,300. The first assumption, together with the second and the third, essentially guarantees that there would be no net saving effect of IRAs. These assumptions, however, are at variance with the empirical evidence, as is the assumption that the promotion of IRAs had no effect on saving behavior.[11]

How individuals in fact behave is an empirical question that cannot be answered by theory alone. Our approach in earlier formal analyses has been to test statistically whether IRAs and other forms of saving are treated as different, without trying to quantify the importance of—or even identify—the possible reasons. We have developed and estimated an econometric specification that encompasses both possibilities—permitting flexible substitution. In particular, a special case of the specification is the perfect-substitutes possibility. This constraint is strongly rejected by the data.[12]

Even less extreme substitution implies that other saving should increase once the IRA limit has been reached. But this pattern is not observed in the data that we have analyzed, suggesting little substitution.[13]

As emphasized above, the simple theory leaves no role for the effect of advertising and other forms of promotion on IRA saving. While it is difficult to quantify the effect of advertising, we are convinced that the promotion played an important role in establishing the popularity of IRAs. To the extent that the promotion was successful, it would show up in our formal analysis as a preference for IRA saving over other forms of saving and as a rejection of the perfect-substitutes assumption, as the data indicate.

The CES data discussed above provide an informal picture very comparable to the results of the formal analysis that was based on the same CES data.[14] Indeed a general test of the behavioral validity of the model used in that analysis was to predict the saving behavior of households in the pre-IRA period, using model estimates based on post-1982 data. In effect, with reference to table 8–1, the model predicted quite accurately the low non-IRA saving in 1980, based on estimates in later years when total saving, including both IRA and non-IRA saving, was much higher. That is, the model predicted well what saving would be if the IRA limit were set to zero.

Within a framework that allows for any degree of substitution between IRA and non-IRA saving and controlling for age, income, other personal characteristics, and accumulated housing and financial assets, the analysis asks whether persons who save more in the form of IRAs in a particular year save less in other finanicial asset forms. Given age and income, accumulated financial assets are used to control for "individual-specific" saving effects. The analysis of course accounts for the explicit limit on IRA contributions and places substantial emphasis on the change in non-IRA saving after the IRA limit is reached.

To find that IRAs and other saving are not perfect substitutes is not anomalous but rather is consistent with other empirical findings on saving behavior. For example, one might expect that persons with firm pension plans would have lower balances in personal financial assets than persons without firm plans, controlling for personal attributes such as age and income. It might be presumed that the firm pension benefits would substitute for personal saving. But the data do not show this. On the contrary, those with firm pensions have higher personal financial asset balances.[15] The data do seem to suggest, however, that firm pensions reduce earnings by inducing earlier departure from the labor force. Instead of pension benefits substituting for personal saving, they

74

may instead—by inducing earlier retirement—substitute for personal earnings.[16]

Closer to the IRA issue itself, it was presumed that IRAs would be more likely to be opened by persons without private pension plans, controlling for personal attributes like income, age, and other financial asset balances. But the data do not show this tendency either; again, the IRA does not appear to be a substitute for firm pension plans.[17]

We find that the simple model—the basis for much of the skepticism about the saving effect of IRAs—provides a poor description of actual IRA saving behavior. Simple economic theory provides an incomplete guide to saving behavior in other instances as well. Thus it should not be surprising if it were misleading in this instance. The primary tool of the simple theory is the rate of return.[18] But the empirical evidence on balance shows little relationship between saving and observed rates of return. Other factors apparently swamp whatever the effect of the return on new saving may be.[19] Personal saving rates vary dramatically among countries, but standard theory does not explain why. A plausible explanation is that habits, cultural norms, "taste" for saving, and the psychology of saving vary from country to country, but they are not incorporated in standard models.

Finally, I believe there are two reasons why IRAs have been so popular. First, one cannot overestimate the effect of the promotion of IRAs, especially near tax time, and especially before the 1986 changes in the IRA rules. Second, the up-front deduction has probably been critical in encouraging IRA saving. That is, even though economic reasoning suggests that the up-front deduction is no different from a back-loaded IRA, from a purely economic perspective, in my view real people find them very different. Some evidence of this may be drawn from experience with the Personal Equity Plan (PEP) in the United Kingdom. The UK plan is patterned after the IRA, but it pertains to equity assets and it is back-loaded. Contributions are from after-tax income, but no tax is paid thereafter—in particular, not when the funds are withdrawn. Anecdotal evidence suggests that financial institutions have found it much more difficult to market the back-loaded PEP than the front-loaded U.S. IRA.

Thus there is considerable motivation to look more broadly for explanations of saving behavior. Relaxation of the restrictive assumptions of the simple model is a start. But the data presented here suggest that a realistic explanation of saving must recognize much broader economic and psychological determinants of individual saving decisions.

9

Examining the Evidence on IRAs and Household Saving

William G. Gale and John Karl Scholz

For the past thirty years the U.S. net national saving rate has been consistently lower than for other Organization for Economic Cooperation and Development countries. Moreover, it has declined steadily over this period, from 9.8 percent in 1960–1967 to 3.7 percent in 1980–1987. In comparison, the Japanese saving rate declined from 21.2 percent to 17.6 percent and the European OECD saving rate fell from 15.6 percent to 9.1 percent over the same periods.[1] While all net national saving rates have fallen, the size of the U.S. decline, 62 percent, is considerably larger than either the 17 percent Japanese decline or the 41 percent European-OECD decline. An extensive academic and public policy literature has examined these trends. Yet the sharp drop in U.S. saving rates in the 1980s, along with the perception that U.S. economic leadership is gradually being eroded in the world economy, has once again placed the spotlight on the role of tax policy in promoting saving.

Several current policy proposals draw their inspiration from individual retirement accounts (IRAs), which were initiated in 1974 to help workers without pension plans save for retirement. IRAs featured tax-deductible contributions up to an annual limit, tax-free accrual of interest, and substantial penalties for early withdrawal before the ac-

We gratefully acknowledge the work of Robert Avery and Arthur Kennickell in developing a cleaned copy of the 1983–1986 Survey of Consumer Finances and in providing extensive documentation. Portions of this project were supported by financial assistance from the LaFollette Institute of Public Affairs, University of Wisconsin–Madison, and the Center for American Politics and Public Policy, U.C.L.A.

count holder reached the age of 59.5. In 1981, as part of an effort to stimulate aggregate saving, IRA eligibility was extended to all taxpayers and annual contribution limits were raised. In 1986 the tax-deductibility of contributions was curtailed. Current proposals, such as the Bush administration's family savings accounts (FSAs) or the Bentsen-Roth "super-IRA," would reverse the direction of the 1986 reforms by implementing new IRA-like saving incentives.[2]

A number of descriptive papers examine the use of IRAs during the period of universal IRA eligibility, 1982—1986.[3] A different, somewhat more technical literature, develops and implements rigorous tests that examine the issue of whether increases in IRA limits over this period would have increased household saving. Daniel R. Feenberg and Jonathan Skinner, William G. Gale and John Karl Scholz, Douglas H. Joines and James G. Manegold, and Steven F. Venti and David A. Wise all address this issue.[4]

For reasons of tractability, much of the debate over the efficacy of IRAs has been carried out using descriptive data. Unfortunately, statements made about these data are occasionally misleading, so we first present what we regard as the facts and implications that can be drawn from the descriptive data. We then briefly describe the formal empirical evidence that is presented in Gale and Scholz.[5]

What Do We Learn from the Descriptive Evidence?

The typical American household saves little. Using data from the 1983–1986 Survey of Consumer Finances (SCF), collected by the Board of Governors of the Federal Reserve in conjunction with other federal agencies, Gale and Scholz show that the median household in 1985 had a combined total of $3,000 of assets in checking and saving accounts, money market funds, certificates of deposit, stocks, bonds, and mutual funds.[6] We refer to these assets collectively as non-IRA financial assets (NIFA). Many others, including Martin Feldstein and Daniel R. Feenberg and Venti and Wise have presented similar evidence.[7]

The argument is occasionally made that because the median household has so little savings, IRA contributions cannot be financed by transferring funds from other existing accounts. The problem with this reasoning is that the median household is in significantly different financial circumstances that the typical IRA contributor. Gale and Scholz show that half of all positive IRA contributions between 1983 and 1985 were made by households with NIFA in excess of $20,000.[8] In addition, the median NIFA of IRA contributors is nine times that of noncontributors. Therefore, the fact that the typical household saves little does not imply that IRA contributions represent an increase in national saving.

There is much heterogeneity in the population when microdata on saving are examined. The fact that the median IRA contributor is considerably wealthier than the typical noncontributor is one example of heterogeneity. A second example is relevant to the formal econometric analyses of IRAs, which examine the effect on saving of raising the annual contribution limit between 1982 and 1986. When examining this policy, an important descriptive issue is to know the asset holdings of the typical IRA limit contributor since it is limit contributors who would be directly affected by an increase in contribution limits. Gale and Scholz show that the typical household constrained by the limit over a three-year period has about twenty times the non-IRA financial assets as the typical household without an IRA.[9] Thus, it should be clear that the typical limit contributor is in different financial circumstances than the typical household. When examining the descriptive data on IRAs, it is important to focus on the relevant set of households and keep in mind the following fact: households that save tend to save in all forms.

Other existing asset balances do not appear to be cannibalized to finance IRA contributions. Feenberg and Skinner show that the non-IRA saving of IRA contributors was higher from 1982 to 1984 than the non-IRA saving of households that did not contribute, even after controlling for initial wealth levels.[10] Venti and Wise have presented similar results.[11]

This implies that the "naive" substitution hypothesis—that IRA contributions are financed by "reshuffling" previously existing assets in a household's portfolio into an IRA—is unlikely to be true. The findings, however, are entirely consistent with the idea that IRA contributions come mainly from saving that would have been done anyway.

It is difficult to discern the effect of IRAs from aggregate saving rates. Chris Carroll and Lawrence H. Summers point out that the Canadian saving rate rose relative to the American rate when Canada liberalized its tax-deferred retirement saving plan in the 1970s.[12] In the United States, however, the rate of personal saving defined from the national income and product accounts fell during the period when tax-deductible IRA contributions were available to all households, despite the fact that IRAs were a popular form of saving. At the same time, Skinner and Feenberg show that saving rates calculated as the difference in net wealth remained high during 1982–1986 and dropped off slightly after 1987.[13] They conclude that "it is difficult to make any conclusions about the effect of IRAs and saving based only on an examination of aggregate saving rates since alternative measures of saving tell such different stories."[14]

We conclude that all of the descriptive evidence presented in the literature to date is consistent with both (1) the view that IRAs are largely financed by shifting public and private saving that would have otherwise occurred and (2) the view that IRA contributions are largely net increments to saving. These two views span the range of positions taken in the literature about the efficacy of IRAs in stimulating saving. Therefore one cannot judge whether IRAs stimulate saving based solely on descriptive data.

Standard economic theory provides an important framework for assessing the ability of IRA-type proposals to increase household saving.[15] These effects are summarized in the following paragraph.

Conventional economic theory implies that IRAs are unlikely to stimulate much additional saving for households that find IRAs to be good substitutes for other types of saving. In theory, capped subsidies for saving will reduce saving for households saving more than the subsidized amount, while there will be opposing income and substitution effects for households saving less than the contribution limit.

The principal statutory feature that distinguishes IRAs from other types of saving is the early withdrawal penalty on IRAs. The early withdrawal penalty, however, does not apply to households when the account holder is 59.5 years old or older. In addition, the more a household has in non-IRA financial assets, the less likely that the household would be forced to pay the early withdrawal penalty. To the extent the early withdrawal penalty does not apply, IRAs should be very good substitutes for other forms of saving. Thus, one preliminary way to examine the effects of IRAs or the effects of limit changes on household saving is to look at what type of households contribute to the IRA limit. In the SCF, more than 35 percent of all households with IRAs have more than $40,000 of non-IRA financial assets or are 59 years old or older. More than 50 percent of the households that were constrained by the IRA limit between 1983 and 1985 were 59 or older or had more than $40,000 of non-IRA financial assets. Thus, for many households, and for limit contributors in particular, IRAs may be good substitutes for other forms of saving.

The Gale and Scholz Model

Because of the ambiguities of the descriptive results, we developed a formal model of IRAs and other saving to analyze the effect of limit changes on household saving.[16] This model is used to motivate the empirical specification we estimate. In the model, saving decisions are derived explicitly from the maximization of a utility function that depends only on current and expected future consumption. In the first two periods (of the three-period optimization problem) households allocate income between consumption, IRA saving, and other saving. IRAs are tax-deductible and have a higher rate of return than other saving when held to the third period.[17] If IRAs are liquidated in the second period, IRAs receive a lower rate of return than other forms of saving. In this way our model incorporates the early withdrawal penalty on IRAs. IRA contribution limits are also incorporated in the model; households are allowed to contribute up to $\$L$ to an IRA. Thus, the model captures the important institutional features of IRAs: the annual contribution limit, the penalty for early withdrawal, and the higher rate of return offered on IRAs through tax-free accumulation of interest and tax-deductible contributions.

Using the framework described above and assuming a quadratic utility function yield closed form equations for IRA saving and other saving in three different situations: the household has no desired IRA saving, has a desired IRA saving between $\$0$ and $\$L$ or has a desired IRA saving that equals or exceeds the maximum contribution limit, $\$L$. For households that contribute the maximum to an IRA, the model allows excess desired IRA saving to spill over into other forms of saving or consumption. The model also allows for heterogeneity in saving behavior by allowing the coefficients on the other saving equations to differ between households that do and do not hold IRAs.

For each of the three types of households—noncontributors, interior IRA contributors, and limit contributors—we simultaneously estimate IRA and non-IRA saving equations that are consistent with the theoretical model. In the empirical implementation of the model, we estimate IRA and other saving between 1983 and 1985 as a function of standard variables, including (in 1983): a constant, age, income, education, non-IRA financial assets, debt, net worth, family size, and dummy variables indicating whether the household had a pension or was married. These variables correspond closely to specifications commonly used to examine saving behavior and previous studies of IRAs.[18] Parameters in this model are identified through the functional form of the estimating equations, which come from the theoretical model.[19]

When estimating this system, we focus primarily on the coefficient that indicates the degree of substitutability between IRA and non-IRA saving. Our estimates imply that increasing the IRA contribution limit in 1983–1985 would have produced little, if any, new net national saving. Most of the increased IRA contributions would have come from reductions in funds that would have been saved anyway. We also find strong statistical evidence that households with IRAs differ systematically from households without IRAs in observed determinants of saving behavior. This implies that tests of the effects of IRAs on the level of saving that depend on comparisons between IRA contributors and noncontributors are not valid, at least in the context of our model.

Our results differ significantly from the formal econometric results of Venti and Wise. While a range of estimates are reported in our work, all of our estimates suggest that IRAs and other forms of saving are more highly substitutable than previous results in the literature. This implies, therefore, that while increases in IRA limits between 1983 and 1985 would have increased IRA contributions by limit contributors, these contributions would largely have been funded by saving that would have been done anyway.

Nontraditional Factors Associated with IRAs

Several authors have emphasized the possibility that nonrational factors might affect IRA decisions. One such argument is that heavy advertising played an important role in making IRAs so popular. Our formal econometric results are consistent both with a standard microeconomic analysis of the effect of a capped subsidy on saving and with much of the empirical evidence about the lack of responsiveness of saving to the aftertax rate of return. Since our empirical results tend to be consistent with these previous results, we see less reason to turn to the nontraditional explanations for IRA behavior.

Having said that, we do not want to underemphasize the possible importance of advertising in affecting the composition, as opposed to the level, of saving from 1982 to 1986. IRAs were a popular form of saving over that period, accounting for approximately 25 percent of all personal saving from 1982 to 1986. Advertising may have played a role in this popularity. Even if advertising were important in making IRA decisions, however, this does not imply that advertising caused IRAs to be funded by reductions in consumption. Similarly, the fact that a large number of IRA accounts are purchased on April 15, the last day tax

81

returns can be filed with the Internal Revenue Service, does not by itself mean that these contributions increase national saving. The crucial issue in both these cases and in all the nontraditional approaches to thinking about IRAs is how these contributions are financed. If contributions made on April 15 are financed by canceling the summer vacation, for example, the contribution would increase household saving.[20] If contributions were financed by shifting funds from taxable accounts, or by making smaller subsequent contributions to other financial investments, an April 15 IRA contribution would have little ultimate impact on household saving.

Two other issues arise in the IRA literature. First, many households appear to invest in IRAs as if they were falsely constrained. It appears, for example, that many married couples contribute exactly $2,000 to an IRA, despite the fact that the couple faces either a $2,250 or $4,000 contribution limit, depending on the employment status of the spouse.[21] While intriguing, this finding is consistent with any of a variety of views about the source of IRA contributions.

Second, Richard Thaler has suggested that IRAs may affect saving through their capacity as a self-control mechanism, that is, individuals place funds in IRAs to restrict themselves from consuming those funds in the (near) future because of the early withdrawal penalty associated with IRAs.[22] Self-control theories have offered a number of intriguing insights to several economic issues, but considerably more work remains to demonstrate that self-control is the compelling motive for IRA contributions.[23] We show, for example, that IRA contributors, and in particular limit contributors, hold substantial amounts of other assets and thus appear to understand the benefits of saving and possess the ability to accumulate assets.

Our results are consistent with a different but equally nontraditional theory of saving. If households save to reach a specific target level of wealth, IRAs will unambiguously reduce saving because of the higher interest rates provided by that form of saving.

Conclusion

One must be careful when interpreting the descriptive evidence on IRAs. While there is evidence against the most extreme reshuffling hypothesis—that households simply draw down existing assets to finance their IRAs—no descriptive evidence of which we are aware proves that IRA contributors have significantly lowered their consumption relative to what it would have been in the absence of IRAs.

82

Clearly a puzzle is raised by the disparate formal econometric results found by Gale and Scholz compared with those presented by Venti and Wise. When compared with the Venti and Wise papers, Gale and Scholz develop and estimate a different model, account for a specific type of heterogeneity by basing the estimation results on a comparison of households constrained by the IRA limit with other households that have contributed to IRAs, and use different data that cover a three-year period. Additional work that can reconcile these divergent findings will be valuable.

10

The Elusive Link between IRAs and Saving

Jonathan Skinner

I saw a T-shirt the other day that said, "Statistics means never having to say you are certain." Economists can share that privilege, particularly when it comes to interpreting the evidence on IRAs and saving. Steven Venti and David Wise estimate a structural econometric model implying that IRAs stimulate aggregate saving, while William Gale and Karl Scholz estimate a structural econometric model implying that IRAs do nothing for aggregate saving.[1] I will try to provide some intuition for why they reach opposite conclusions.[2] I will also try to emphasize empirical facts that economists do agree about, and suggest that these facts may play a part in saving behavior.

Let me turn first to the pioneering studies by Venti and Wise. If IRAs were a pure tax dodge, then everyone with a little bit of saving would contribute, especially those who are over age fifty-nine and not subject to a withdrawal penalty if they want to take their money out.[3] Like checking off the personal exemption, a pure tax dodge provides an instant tax rebate without requiring any change in behavior. If IRAs were this simple tax shelter, then they would have no impact on total saving—they would just lose revenue for the U.S. Treasury.

Venti and Wise stress that the degree of substitutability between IRA and non-IRA saving is crucial to determining whether IRAs are new saving. Why should substitutability be so important? I will use an analogy to explain. Suppose that all ice cream is vanilla, and the government introduces a new kind of ice cream. To encourage this new ice cream, they provide a half-price coupon for the first pint purchased. If the new kind of ice cream is just like vanilla, then the two types of ice cream are perfect substitutes. Everyone who buys any ice cream will take the government rebate and buy at least one pint of the new ice cream. Lobbyists for the ice cream industry will claim that ICAs (ice cream accounts) are a great success at stimulating production of new ice cream. But has total ice cream consumption increased? No, consumers have simply reduced their prior purchases of vanilla by one pint to buy the new pint of ice cream; total consumption is unchanged.[4]

Suppose now that the new strain of ice cream is chocolate. Chocolate and vanilla ice cream are imperfect substitutes. Eating an extra pint of chocolate does not cause me to cut back on vanilla by the full pint. (I might even consume more.) Therefore, introducing (and subsidizing) a new flavor of ice cream that is an imperfect substitute for the existing ice cream will stimulate total ice cream production. One empirical implication of imperfect substitutes is that people who strongly prefer vanilla over chocolate will not purchase any chocolate despite the subsidized price. That is, a sizable fraction of the population will never avail themselves of either chocolate ice cream or the government discount.

The analogy carries over in a straightforward way to the Venti and Wise model. Fewer than one-third of all families have purchased an IRA in any year. Even among the prime candidates for IRA accounts, ages fifty-five to sixty-four and income between $50,000 and $75,000, one-third still do not touch IRAs despite the obvious tax advantages. In the context of their model, this finding implies that IRAs are imperfect substitutes for non-IRA saving. Expanding the IRA limits would therefore be predicted to stimulate aggregate saving.

Gale and Scholz question the notion that IRAs are imperfect substitutes. IRAs are not so much a new flavor of ice cream as a less liquid, and hence less desirable, form of saving. Gale and Scholz also suggest that contributors are fundamentally different from noncontributors; contributors hold far more in liquid wealth and receive higher incomes. Allowing for these differences in preferences, as Gale and Scholz do in their model, provides a different explanation for why so many do not contribute to an IRA—they have little taste for any type of saving. Those with a strong taste for saving will save in all kinds of assets, including IRAs. The idea is not that IRAs stimulate saving, but that people who were saving anyway buy IRAs. Had there been no IRAs, according to the Gale and Scholz model, the IRA contributions would have been saved anyway in taxable assets.[5]

While the Gale and Scholz model does provide a more realistic characterization of saving behavior, they also must make strong assumptions to get their results. The problem is that they have a single cross-section of saving behavior and must infer from this snapshot whether IRAs stimulate saving behavior or whether saving tastes cause IRA purchases. One way to sort out this puzzle is to include in the model a variable that affects non-IRA saving but has no effect on IRA saving. To return to our analogy, this task is similar to finding some characteristic of individuals that affects vanilla ice cream but not chocolate ice cream consumption. Such a variable is hard to think of. Gale and Scholz assume that age-squared affects non-IRA saving but does not affect IRA saving. But there is little theoretical reason to expect that this assumption holds.

A second way that they can solve the puzzle is by assuming differences in functional form. To take a simple example, we could assume that IRA saving depends linearly on income while non-IRA saving depends exponentially on income.[6] The problem is that economists know so little about saving behavior, much less about specific functional forms. While this study is an important advance in modeling saving behavior (for a number of other reasons not mentioned here), it is probably too early to tell from these cross-sectional studies whether IRAs stimulate saving.

Experience since 1982

What have we learned about IRAs since 1982 when eligibility was expanded? The first fact is that IRAs were not a simple, costless tax dodge. There were some attempts to make IRAs into a simple tax dodge by, say, suggesting that it be charged to a cedit card ("Short on cash? Not to worry, says S&L, just put it on your credit card," claimed one headline in *American Banker* [February 27, 1985]), but my impression is that such efforts were not entirely successful.

The second fact is that IRAs are new saving in a limited sense: people who bought them were active savers, so they did not have to cash out existing assets to make IRA contributions. Suppose, for example, an indivual had zero saving in 1982 but opened an IRA anyway. Her IRA saving would go up by $2,000, her non-IRA saving would fall by $2,000, and total saving would be zero. This type of person was not the typical IRA contributor. IRA contributors tended to save actively in IRA as well as non-IRA saving.[7] A representative IRA contributor might have saved $5,000 total, with $2,000 going into an IRA fund. This finding establishes that at a minimum, the tax subsidies are at least reaching the fairly small fraction of families who are active savers.[8] The much harder question is whether the taxpayer would have saved the entire $5,000 anyway in the absence of the IRA, in which case IRAs would have done nothing to stimulate saving.

The third aspect of IRAs that has emerged in recent years is that taxpayers buy IRAs late in the tax season, and they tend to buy them when they have underwithheld their tax payments. By April 14, few (legal) ways of reducing taxable income for the prior year remain. IRAs were a popular last-minute gambit; in the 1983 tax year, for example, 39 pecent of all contributions were made in 1984, presumably before the April 15 filing date.[9] Also, if the taxpayer owed the IRS more than it had withheld, he was much more likely to contribute to an IRA, holding constant factors such as income, wealth, and filing status.[10]

The lateness of IRA contributions could be interpreted as a desire to fine-tune tax planning after the tax year is over. The propensity to contribute to IRAs when the taxpayer is underwithheld could be attributed to aggresive tax planners who both underwithhold (as a strategy to earn interest on the unpaid taxes) and defer taxes with IRAs. My own view is that these factors are supportive of the view that IRAs are as much a psychological as an economic decision. These two findings are also consistent with the notion that taxpayers would rather pay money into an IRA account than write a check to the IRS at tax-filing time.

These findings in no sense prove that IRAs are new saving. The last-minute IRA contributions could be shuffled (old) saving rather than new additions to the saving pool. But even if the IRA conribution is made from a Visa card, there is a large difference between the short-term credit card debt (with an 18 percent incentive to pay off the debt!) and a locked-in longterm IRA saving account.

To summarize, there is a continuing debate over the impact on saving of the IRA program. The two best-known econometric models yield different conclusions, leading to some uncertainty about whether IRAs are effective at stimulating the national saving rate. There is also some evidence that the up-front deduction provided a psychological impetus to save, suggesting that orthodox econometric models may be unable to capture adequately individual motivations for saving.[11]

IRAs have sometimes been suggested as a cure for the low saving rate in the United States. Suppose we take an extreme position and assume that all IRA saving is new saving. IRAs never amounted to more than 1.2 percent of disposable income. So they are unlikely by themselves to cure the 3–4 percent decline in national saving rates. If they are a cure for anything, they may be better at the original motivation for introducing them in the first place—to assist American families to provide for their retirement. As Venti and Wise have shown, the median liquid wealth of families nearing retirement is $6,600. Clearly a few years of IRA contributions could have an important impact on the financial position of elderly households.

PART FOUR

Economic and Social Goals of Tax Policy

11

Is It Time to Abandon Tax Reform?

Joel B. Slemrod

Most of the tax policy changes now being debated fall into three categories: first, saving incentives, including the expanded individual retirement account (IRA), the super IRA, and family savings accounts (FSA); second, capital gains tax cuts; and third, child credits, perhaps financed by increases in top bracket rates.

What all these proposals have in common is that they represent a retreat from the spirit that infused the Tax Reform Act of 1986. That spirit was the desirability of a broad-based tax system with low rates, one that removes, as much as possible, the tax system from the allocation of resources and private decision making.

Five years after the passage of the Tax Reform Act of 1986, why are we debating different ways to make this retreat? Why are there no proposals in a fourth category that further lowers rates by broadening the base and removing the tax system even further from market decisions? Not for any good reason.

Will these proposals work in the way they are supposed to, and are they worth supporting? Let me first give quick answers to these questions, and then I'll provide some support for my responses.

Saving Incentives

First consider saving incentives of the IRA variety. Although the evidence is not conclusive, in my opinion they mostly induce a switching of assets and they do not generate much new net saving.

Concerning capital gains tax reduction, yes, reducing the tax on capital gains will reduce the cost of equity capital, although not only for American corporations. Arguably this ought to be lowered, but reducing the tax on capital gains is a blunt instrument for achieving this goal. Preferential capital gains taxation leads to great complexity in the tax system. In fact some tax lawyers have argued, regarding the pre-1986 tax reform system, that half the complexity of the tax system was due to the differential treatment of capital gains and other forms of capital income. It is a complexity-breeding way to lower the cost of equity capital.

Concerning refundable child credits, I recommend never to listen to economists on issues of fairness. Economists are trained to measure the economic costs of enforcing a more or less progressive system of taxation, but they have no comparative or absolute advantage in judging one system fairer than another, or even in deciding how to trade off any benefits from a more equal distribution of income against the costs of these changes. For this reason I will not come down one way or the other on distributional grounds. On incentive grounds, I do not think there is any strong argument for refundable child credits.

Let me explain why I believe there is no reason now to debate *how* to retreat from the spirit of the 1986 tax bill. First, here are some bad reasons to support a policy.

Bad reason number one is that other countries are different. One form of this argument is that because we save less than other countries we have to change our fiscal system to save more. We also watch less soccer on television than any other country; in fact we probably watch less soccer than we did ten years ago. Stated another way, our capital gains tax rate is higher than any other country's, so we should lower it. It is true that we are on the high end of the range of capital gains taxation, but our corporate tax rate is lower than that of just about any of our major trading partners. Should we raise that up to the average? My point is that policy should not be made by picking and choosing one particular tax rate or provision and comparing it with some other country's; this is a very selective and imprecise method.

Bad reason number two for supporting a policy change is to make a comparison with the past. The current example of that is arguing that the personal exemption allowance, or an equivalent refundable child credit, ought to be increased because in real terms it is not much lower than it was forty years ago. Why was it necessarily right forty years ago? The top marginal tax rate was then over 90 percent, in part to finance the higher real personal exemption allowances. Do we want to use the same argument to go back to the 90 percent plus top rates?

This kind of argument begs the question of whether we had it right or wrong in the good old days. We save less than we did in the 1970s, but then, a lot of other aggregate statistics would look quite different now from the way they looked twenty years ago. There is a legitimate argument that our saving rate is too low, and we should think about changing certain aspects of our tax system that lead to low saving. For example, if we believe the source of a too-low saving rate is the double taxation of dividends, then it makes sense that to alleviate that problem, instead of thinking about a capital gains cut, we should think seriously about integrating the personal and corporate tax systems to eliminate the double taxation of dividends.

Child Credits

I will turn to the child credit program as an incentive program. To measure the ability to pay correctly so that tax burdens are allocated fairly across families, an exemption allowance or a deduction—not a credit—is appropriate. If the child credit is to be a pronatalist policy because we think it is appropriate national policy to promote population growth, then it is problematic for the credit not only to promise money to families who are contemplating expanding but also to transfer money to families who already have children. This argument should be familiar to veterans of the debate between an investment tax credit and a lowered corporate tax rate. The former provides tax relief only to new capital; the latter provides it to both new and old capital. Child credits provide tax relief to "old" children as well as "new" children, to borrow the analogy. The present value of the tax relief to existing children of some of these proposals is on the order of $250 billion. So if it is meant to be a pronatalist policy, and if these are the kinds of incentives we want, then this is not a well-targeted policy. It is not targeted at poor families with children. The suggestion of the National Commission on Children report to expand the Head Start program is more on target.

Why Abandon Tax Reform?

All three categories of the tax proposals have one common feature: they are a retreat from the spirit of the Tax Reform Act of 1986, a low rate, broad-base tax system that minimizes interference of the tax system in the allocation of resources.

Some of the proposals explicitly pay for their generosity by increasing taxes elsewhere. The Gore-Downey proposals are such an example, and their forthrightness should be commended. Other proposals leave open the question of how the tax incentives will be financed. But generosity to some people and some activities increases either the rate of taxes on others or the deficit.

So why are we contemplating *how* to retreat from the Tax Reform Act of 1986? What has caused the abandonment of the principle that, to everyone's surprise, swept tax reform into law in 1986? Politically, the answer in part is the age-old urge to reward identifiable constituencies and the age-old urge to do something rather than nothing.

The answer definitely is *not* that the Tax Reform Act of 1986 has proved to be a failure. The prognostications of the doomsayers about the bill—that it would lead to the deindustrialization of America, for example—have clearly been proved wrong. At least until the recent recession, real investment had been on or above trend since 1986. The personal saving rate had rebounded from a low in 1987 to a rate higher than trend. The tax shelter industry has dried up. Foreign domestic investment, inward and outward, has been rising.

Nor do I believe that the recent recession can be blamed on the tax reform act. More likely, the uncertainty surrounding the gulf crisis and the increased oil prices that accompanied it pushed into recession an economy that had been growing for about eight years.

What have we learned from the years following the Tax Reform Act of 1986, and from the 1980s in general? From the point of view of long-run planning, these major tax changes are the worst possible thing. But from an academic's point of view they are wonderful experiments to help us learn about the effects of tax policy.

We have had two major tax reforms in the 1980s. Maybe they came too close together to enable us to look at the long-run effects of the first, and maybe we are too close to the second to understand its long-run effects. But we cannot resist looking at what the evidence of the last decade teaches us.

Impact of the Tax Reform Act of 1986

The Office of Tax Policy Research at the University of Michigan sponsored a conference designed to evaluate the effects of the Tax Reform Act of 1986. The volume that evolved from that conference is the most systematic and comprehensive analysis of the initial evidence of the effects. My own conclusion based on the research presented at that conference and my own reading of the evidence from the 1980s, is that a hierarchy of decisions are affected by taxation. Decisions at the top are most affected by taxation, those at the bottom are least affected.

At the top of the hierarchy are timing decisions—for example, when to sell capital assets, when to do mergers and acquisitions. Americans respond well to sales, whether at the department store or in the tax system. For example, we saw evidence of an enormous response in the last quarter of 1986 in anticipation of the increase in the capital gains tax rate and the abandonment of the General Utilities doctrine. Many examples show that people are willing to change the timing of transactions in order to take advantage of the tax laws.

At the second level of the hierarchy are financial and accounting decisions. Evidence suggests a significant response to taxation of such things as debt-equity ratios, mergers and acquisitions, and Subchapter S elections.

Third, and at the bottom of the hierarchy, are real decisions. The evidence of the last decade tells us that real investment decisions, real saving decisions, and real labor supply decisions are not easily moved around by the tax system.

My defense of the 1986 bill and its spirit has so far been largely negative. I have argued that the doomsayers have been proved wrong by enumerating all the bad things that have not happened. I cannot point to concrete evidence proving that the Tax Reform Act of 1986 has turned the country around, or that our saving rate is heading toward Japanese levels. But I believe that once the current recession ends, saving, investment, and other indicators of economic growth will start to look very healthy again by recent historical standards.

The evidence concerning one other objective of the tax reform act—to simplify the tax system—is decidedly mixed. In some respects the system seems to have been simplified; in others, it is clearly more complicated.

So much for the lessons of the 1980s; what about the 1990s? The most important change in perspective is the attention given to international considerations. Until now—and even in the 1980s, when the reality of global competition was crystal clear—tax policy has been almost entirely domestically driven.

We were lucky with the Tax Reform Act of 1986 because, even considering global competition, I think that was the right way to go. But we cannot ignore international considerations from now on and hope that our tax policy direction will be right.

The reality of international competition makes the benefits of a low rate, broad-based tax system even greater than they are in a purely domestic economy. One reason for this is that in an international economy the economic cost of distortions introduced by the tax system is even higher than otherwise, because the menu of alternatives is greater. Tax penalties will drive more activity away when there are many alternatives, including alternatives offshore. Tax subsidies, will, in a global economy, be more effective in attracting economic activity, even though the opportunity cost of that activity exceeds its return to the country.

A second reason is that the benefits of the low rate that a broad base allows are even greater in an international context. This is especially clear in the corporate tax case. It is well known that multinational corporations, which more and more are dominating economic activity in the world, have the ability to shift income across jurisdictions. The low, 34 percent rate that a broad corporate tax base allows is a revenue magnet rather than a revenue repellent. Any movement toward a less broad base, which will ultimately force an increase in the tax rate, will turn that around.

We need to understand better the influence of our taxation of foreign-source income on behavior. As an example, consider research and development (R & D). Many economists agree that the government ought to get involved in subsidizing R & D. Because of the nature of spillover benefits from research and development, a corporation or individual may forgo R & D that is not in its private interest but is in the social interest.

How does the tax system treat R & D? First, it allows R & D expenses to be deducted immediately from taxable income rather than amortized. It offers an incremental, nonpermanent, and often ineffective R & D credit. For multinationals it stipulates very complicated rules about the allocation of the parent corporation's R & D expenses to foreign-source income. For many multinationals these allocation rules can be as important as the other two aspects of the tax treatment of R & D in influencing the amount and location of their R & D activity, but they have received much less policy attention than the other two. As multinational operations become increasingly important we must carefully consider whether our apparently domestic tax policies are consistent with the tax incentives that are implicit in how we tax foreign-source income.

My continued support for a streamlined, low-rate tax system does not mean I believe there are no good reasons for government involvement in the economy or that we have now achieved the ideal tax system. For example, I support government subsidy of R & D, and I believe serious consideration of integration of the personal and the corporate tax systems is in order. Finally, I think that we ought to give continued attention to reducing the complexity of the tax system.

Some of my own research suggests that the resource cost of collecting taxes in the United States is now approximately $65 billion a year. Complexity is a tax policy in itself, and a bad tax policy. I applaud what I perceive as more legislative attention to keeping the complexity of the tax system from getting any worse and, ideally, to receiving it.

One important aspect of simplicity is stability of the tax system. Since World War II, there have been more years with a tax bill than years without. Frequent tax changes make long-run planning difficult. They require relearning the rules and the behavior made appropriate by changing tax rules.

Before we change course again and reverse the course of the Tax Reform Act of 1986 to return to a Swiss-cheese based, high-rate system, we ought to renew the debate about the spirit of that bill. The arguments for it are stronger than ever. Before it is abandoned, these arguments must be confronted and refuted.

12

IRAs, Saving, and the Generational Effects of Fiscal Policy

Laurence J. Kotlikoff

The United States is facing a saving crisis. In 1990 our net national saving rate was 2.6 percent. Even if we make corrections for the possible overstatement of depreciation, we still have a national saving rate running at least 50 percent below the national average observed between 1950 and 1979. Over time, this derisory saving behavior will lower our per capita income relative to that of other nations. Indeed, it will not take long for our per capita income to fall dramatically compared with per capita income in Japan and Germany. The U.S. per capita income ranking, which is calculated using the admittedly volatile exchange rates, is now ninth among nations of the world—compare this with its ranking of first in 1976.

I have two goals for this essay. First I will indicate my views concerning the efficacy of IRAs and FSAs for promoting additional national saving. Second, I will focus on the government's generational policy and point out the dangers for national saving of continuing the course of policy that has for the past four decades transferred huge amounts of resources toward contemporary old generations and away from contemporary young generations and those not yet born. An important part of my message concerning generational policy will be that the federal government's budget deficit is a wholly unreliable measure for understanding how we are treating different cohorts of Americans. To examine generational policy I will rely on generational accounting, which I have developed jointly with Alan Auerbach of the

University of Pennsylvania and Jagadeesh Gokhale of the Cleveland Federal Reserve Bank.[1]

Saving Incentives

Regarding saving incentives, IRAs and FSAs do not represent effective means for increasing national saving.[2] Indeed, the national saving rate declined at precisely the time IRAs were introduced.

From a theoretical perspective, IRAs and FSAs represent one of the worst ways imaginable to design a saving incentive. These policies provide windfalls to a large number of households—particularly rich, upper-income ones—while providing no marginal incentive for these households to consume less and save more. These windfalls induce more current consumption, which reduces national saving. For lower-income households that do not receive an effective windfall through the tax arbitrage opportunities of these so-called saving incentives, these schemes provide some incentive to save and to consume less because of the price or substitution effect. But they provide an offsetting incentive to dissave—that is, consume more—because of an income effect.

In studying the consumption effects of IRAs one would ideally want to understand how each household is affected by the IRAs—that is, to understand which households receive windfalls but have no greater incentive to save and which are given increased incentives to save at the margin. One would next want to relate the household-specific impacts of IRAs to the consumption responses of the households. Unfortunately, none of the empirical studies of IRAs have considered how IRAs directly affect households' consumption. Rather than study consumption directly, the existing cross-section studies examine saving.

But measuring saving is notoriously difficult. A major problem with the existing studies in this regard is their failure to control properly for dissaving, or borrowing, in calculating net saving. This is a critical deficiency, given the fact that households can use IRAs to engage in tax arbitrage by taking out larger mortgages, the interest on which is deductible, and then investing the additional funds in IRAs and Keogh accounts that earn tax-free interest. I hope future studies will use the available Bureau of Labor Statistics Survey of Consumer Expenditures to study directly how IRAs in the 1980s affected the consumption of individual households.

In the absence of convincing household evidence of the consumption response to IRAs, one can only fall back on microbased simulation models of the effects of these policies. My dynamic life-cycle simulation model with Alan Auerbach assumes quite significant substitution effects, but it also assumes strong income effects in response to changes in incentives to save.[3]

Simulating the expansion of IRAs in our model reduces national saving, however, because the income effects dominate the substitution effects.[4] Even if we give these saving schemes their best day in court and assume that they provide true incentives at the margin for households to consume less and save more, we still find that the policies reduce national saving because the income effects of the tax break induce consumption to rise by more than the incentive effects induce consumption to fall. If their income effects could be offset, IRA proposals would be more likely to encourage more savings. But if IRA-type policies were expanded, the cost of making up for reduced revenues would most likely be passed on to future generations—with the implication that the positive income effects of such policies enjoyed by current generations would induce additional current consumption.

It should also be pointed out that IRAs and FSAs are really small potatoes. The effects of these policies are simply too insignificant to turn around the national saving problem. We need to devise something more fundamental to really change Americans' saving behavior. And we need to realize that the problem cannot be left primarily to the federal government. Rather than try to bribe Americans to save more, the federal government needs to explain to the public in concrete terms the dire consequences for them personally and nationally of the failure to save.

Governmental Generational Policy

To illustrate my analysis of the generational policy we have been running in the United States during the past forty years I will construct a simple equation—$A + B + C = D$—which I call the government's intertemporal budget constraint. The letter A stands for the present value of the government's spending on goods and services. That spending has to be paid for either by B, C, or D, where

B = government's current net assets
C = the present value of remaining lifetime net tax payments—taxes paid less transfers received—of current generations
D = present value of lifetime net tax payments of generations not yet born

100

Intuitively we know that if the government cannot cover its time path of spending on goods and services from its available net assets plus payments through time by current generations, then future generations will have to pay for the balance. My coauthors and I have calculated values for A, B, and C and used the equation to determine the value of D, the burden to be foisted on our posterity. The arithmetic is quite straightforward, but the calculations are detailed and certain results are sensitive to assumptions about the discount rate, future productivity growth, changes in the age distribution, and so on.

We have calculated baseline numbers for present values of lifetime net payments for members of the total current population. We express these numbers as payments per person and not as the total sum of the payments. According to our calculations, for example, to finance the present value of government spending on goods and services, forty-year-old males can expect to pay about $176,000. A seventy-year-old male, however, can expect to pay a negative amount—to receive $42,700. This difference reflects the fact that such older males will receive more in payments from the government, primarily in the form of social security benefits, than they can expect to pay in taxes. Our analysis of the net present value of payments of those currently alive (current generations) is consistent with the National Income and Product Accounts data on taxes and transfers.

Application of our formula, after making these calculations, indicates that those Americans not yet born will experience a 21 percent greater lifetime burden of payments than the total lifetime burden of the youngest members of the current population. On average, new members of the next generation will inherit a payment obligation with a present value almost $12,000 higher than that for the youngest members of the current generation. This payment obligation will grow slowly in present value terms for people born in the more distant future. All these calculations of course, are made under the assumption that current tax and spending policies will remain unchanged. I should also note that the 21 percent greater lifetime burden to be imposed on future generations is quite robust with respect to the rates of discount and economic growth assumed.

In table 12–1 I present some of the effects of the changes in generational policy over the past four decades. The numbers in table 12–1 show the hypothetical effects of starting with the results generated by policies in effect in 1989 and then imposing the policies of the previous decades to modify policies currently in place. That is, instead of tracing the historical effects of policy changes, these comparisons

101

TABLE 12–1
HYPOTHETICAL EFFECTS OF IMPOSING POLICIES OF DIFFERENT
DECADES ON 1989 GENERATIONAL ACCOUNTS, 1950–1990
(thousands of dollars)

	1950s	1950s, with no change in govt. spending	1960s	1970s	1980s
Males					
Ages					
0	15.8	4.1	7.8	7.9	5.3
10	23.4	5.5	12.2	12.2	7.4
20	32.6	6.8	15.8	14.3	7.3
30	35.8	3.5	16.1	12.5	4.4
40	32.0	−1.9	12.3	7.1	−.7
50	21.3	−8.7	3.9	−2.8	−7.5
60	6.6	−15.3	−6.0	−13.8	−12.0
70	2.5	−10.3	−4.8	−9.7	−9.0
80	2.8	−4.4	−1.3	−3.7	−5.5
Future generations	15.0	3.6	6.6	7. 2	−1.2
Females					
Ages					
0	12.1	4.0	.1	.0	4.4
10	17.8	5.7	1.0	.5	6.1
20	23.1	6.2	2.4	.0	6.1
30	21.2	1.6	2.9	−1.8	4.8
40	16.8	−3.6	1.2	−4.9	2.1
50	8.4	−10.2	−4.2	−11.7	−2.8
60	−1.7	−16.3	−10.9	−19.3	−7.0
70	−2.7	−12.3	−9.0	−15.5	−6.1
80	−.2	−5.4	−4.2	−7.9	−3.7
Future generations	12.5	4.3	−1.2	−1.2	1.5

SOURCE: Laurence J. Kotlikoff, *Generational Accounts—Knowing Who Pays, and When, for What We Spend* (New York, N.Y.: The Free Press, 1992).

102

examine the policies of each decade separately, using the results for
1989 as a point of reference. In the column labeled 1970s, for example,
we see what would happen if, in addition to the policies in place now,
we added the policies of the 1970s. We see that the policy changes of
the 1970s were quite good for older generations. For example, a male
aged sixty would receive about $13,800 in present value terms from
adding those policies of the 1970s; a newborn male, by contrast, would
lose $7,900. In addition to the increased present value of net payment
obligations that accrued to younger members of the current population,
new members of the next generation of males also lost $7,200.

The policies of the 1960s were similar to those of the 1970s in that
they benefited older members of the population at the expense of younger
members. The policies of the 1950s increased net tax payments for
almost everybody, primarily because the government's spending on
goods and services rose dramatically from about 14 percent of output to
about 22 percent of output over the course of that decade.

Despite this sharp increase in net tax obligations for most members
of the population living then, the growth in future spending built into
these policy changes left future generations much worse off—by $15,000
for males and by $12,500 for females. If we abstract from government
spending policies, it is apparent from column 2 that the policies of the
1950s, like those of the subsequent three decades, also involved a great
deal of redistribution toward older generations and away from younger
generations.

The federal deficit relative to GNP rose dramatically in the 1980s,
but in the previous decades the ratio of federal debt to GNP actually
declined, despite the increases in the fiscal burden that were being
placed on future generations. In the 1950s and 1960s the ratio of federal
debt to GNP declined very dramatically. The main reason for the rise in
the burden on future generations despite the decline in the debt-to-GNP
ratio is that the redistribution in the 1950s, 1960s, and 1970s was in
large part associated with expansion of unfunded social security and
Medicare payment obligations.

If we continue to focus on the federal deficit as our gauge of
generational policy then we can easily continue to miss most of the
generational policy action. The 1950s, 1960s, and 1970s were periods
when the debt-to-GNP ratio declined dramatically; but at the same time
we had substantial redistribution toward older people at the expense of
younger and future generations. When federal debt went up in the 1980s
we also had significant redistribution among age groups in the population, but the burden on future generations remained about the same. It

was reduced slightly for males and increased by about the same amount for females. Those who bore most of the burden of the policies of the 1980s were today's children, not tomorrow's.

Proposals for the Future

To turn around our saving situation we need to bring our generational policy into balance. We have to come up with policies to reduce the $67,000 burden (about $89,500 for males and $44,200 for females) that current policies impose on future generations. We need to lower their burden and raise the burden on ourselves. The kind of accounting I have outlined can help us understand how we are treating future generations. It is not perfect, and certainly it requires making many assumptions, but it provides us with a structure for thinking systematically about how we are treating future generations.

Our national saving rate is as low as it is because the government has passed the generational buck for four decades. It has given money to older generations, either in the form of direct transfers or of reduced tax payments, and it has handed the bill for these giveaways to young and future generations. Baby boomers intuitively understand why they are not saving very much—it is because their taxes are so high. They do not have much money left to save significant amounts after they have paid their taxes.

Focusing only on current federal budget deficits can mislead us about implications of policy changes for future generations. In table 12–2 I describe two different policy changes and their effects, based on our generational accounting method. The first column in table 12–2 shows the generational impacts of a hypothetical five-year reduction by 20 percent in federal income taxes. After the five years taxes are raised again, in order to maintain the higher ratio of debt to GNP as constant from that point on.

This policy would benefit existing older generations and even some baby boomers. But it would increase the present value of net payments that need to be made by our children. It would also impose a higher burden on our grandchildren and our descendants beyond that.

Now compare column 1 with column 2, which reflects the results of an increase in social security benefits by 20 percent and a rise in payroll taxes to finance that on a continual basis—that is, more pay-as-you-go finance. The differential impact among age groups in the current population is much greater than it is for the temporary income tax reduction considered in column 1. For sixty-year-olds, for example, the

104

TABLE 12–2

CHANGES IN GENERATIONAL ACCOUNTS DUE TO TWO HYPOTHETICAL
POLICIES

(thousands of dollars)

	5-Year Tax Cut[a]	Social Security Benefit Increase[b]
Males		
Ages		
0	1.6	2.7
10	2.6	3.9
20	1.7	5.3
30	.3	4.8
40	−2.2	2.0
50	−3.5	−3.1
60	−3.8	−10.4
70	−2.0	−10.5
80	−1.2	−6.0
Future generations	1.5	3.1
Females		
Ages		
0	.8	1.0
10	1.4	1.5
20	.4	1.8
30	.2	.7
40	−.8	−1.2
50	−1.5	−4.7
60	−1.6	−10.0
70	−1.1	−10.0
80	−.7	−6.4
Future generations	.8	1.1

a. This column represents a hypothetical five-year reduction in federal income taxes of 20 percent.
b. This column represents the results of an increase in social security benefits by 20 percent.
SOURCE: Laurence J. Kotlikoff, *Generational Accounts—Knowing Who Pays, and When, for What We Spend* (New York, N.Y.: The Free Press, 1992).

105

social security benefit increase entails a windfall of about $10,000, compared with a windfall that averages about $2,700 in the first column.

The burden on future generations is increased a great deal more under the pay-as-you-go tax and benefits change analyzed in column 2 than under the temporary tax cut in column 1—$3,100 versus $1,500 for males. The policy that generates the results in column 2, however, would not occur from any change in the federal budget deficit, as we conventionally measure it. Under the policy with the results reported in column 1, the federal debt would rise during the course of five years by about three-quarters of a trillion dollars. The underlying reason, of course, is that future obligations are reportedly explicit in the temporary tax cut case, while future social security obligations do not appear in our conventional budget accounts.

These comparisons show that if we continue to look only at the conventionally measured budget deficit of the federal government we will continue to miss much of the picture—with respect to both generational equity and the likely effects of fiscal policy on U.S. saving. We really need some kind of meaningful generational accounting analysis in order to understand how we are treating different age groups in our current population and generations yet to come.

What can the government do right now to raise U.S. saving or at least prevent its further decline? The most important step is for the government to adopt policies that improve generational balance. Attaining generational balance or at least forestalling greater imbalance requires getting an immediate handle on the expansion of Medicare costs. These costs continue to rise, and the burden of paying for additional expenditures will not be visited on the recipients of the additional Medicare transfers—rather, it will be on today's baby boomers and their children. Unfortunately, because no cash-flow financing crisis is immediately expected in Medicare, we will probably wait until the turn of the century to bring Medicare growth under control. But that waiting could by itself more than double the present generational imbalance.

To help achieve generational balance the government needs to do a generational accounting of the consequences of any major piece of fiscal legislation. Congress now systematically looks at the implications of its policy initiatives for the cross-sectional distribution of income. It should also examine the implications of its policies for the intergenerational distribution of income. Showing the generational implications of policy proposals entails an effort similar to that necessary for putting together income distribution tables. The argument that generational accounting

106

is too complex or time-consuming for practical application is bogus.

Another low-cost step the government could take is to mobilize individual households into thinking carefully about how much they are saving. It could send each household an annual statement saying, "Here's how much your household has contributed to social security. Here's what we calculate your future social security benefits to be, based on your current and past contributions. Here's how much you earn, and here's how much you should be saving either on your own or through your employer to ensure a reasonable amount of savings in old age."

If each of us got such a statement annually our attention would be caught and perhaps our psychology of saving, which is in such urgent need of redress, would really change.

13

Tax Policy and Income Distribution

Wendell E. Primus

The Gore-Downey bill would replace the personal exemption for children under eighteen with an $800 refundable tax credit. The cost of this refundable credit would be financed by increasing income taxes on the richest 5 percent of American families, with the overwhelming portion of the revenue increases occurring on the richest 1 percent of the population. The Gore-Downey tax credit is phased in with earnings, and it equals the higher of $400 per family or 20 percent of earned income, up to $800 per child. By competing for scarce dollars that could be devoted to expanding individual retirement accounts (IRAs) or to reducing the capital gains tax rate, it therefore fits into any discussion of personal saving and consumption.

Middle-Income Tax Relief

I begin with the proposition that the Gore-Downey bill does as much for savings as the IRA bills, simply because Gore-Downey is paid for and does not increase the federal deficit. Until the authors of the IRA bills indicate precisely how their proposals will be paid for, we have only one-half of the equation on the table. It is premature to discuss income distribution effects until we have seen both the benefits and the pain of a revenue-neutral proposal.

Furthermore, back-loaded IRAs are a sophisticated way of circumventing the budget rules, which require that all entitlement and mandatory spending increases and revenue losses be completely offset by spending reduction or revenue increases over the next five years. This is analogous to designing a bill to combat child poverty and starting the entitlement increases in year six.

The climate for saving improved significantly during the 1980s. Real interest rates increased from what they had been in the 1960s and 1970s. The income of the top quintile, presumably the portion of the population most capable of saving, increased significantly. Despite the meagerness of our savings, the market inefficiently allocated much of them into unproductive investments. We wasted billions of dollars in the real estate market—witness the savings and loan scandal.

What problem are we now trying to solve? What market failure is driving us to intervene in this market to increase the national saving rate? If low economic growth is the primary problem, what we most need is more investment in human capital and improvement in the quality of the labor force—not more investment in real estate, particularly commercial, retail, and large single family dwellings.

Income Distributional Effects

The change in the distribution of income over time is really a scorecard on governmental policy and how the economy is working. Over the past years two changes have occurred that will make income distribution an issue for many years. First, during the 1970s and 1980s, income inequality grew significantly, particularly among the richest 1 or 5 percent of the population, creating the policy question, What should government do about its growth?

Second, the Joint Committee on Taxation (JCT) assembled a tax and income model that examines the entire federal tax structure. One can model changes in any part of the tax structure (except for corporate taxes) and examine the income distributional effects of that tax change. The Congressional Budget Office (CBO) went one step further; during the budget summit it implemented a microsimulation tool that modeled changes in federal spending programs and revenue changes and then examined them on households with varying incomes.

By comparing several sets of federal governmental policy changes, one can determine which set is more progressive. These institutional changes at both JCT and CBO will forever influence tax and entitlement spending debates on Capitol Hill.

When comparing the income distribution of the population in 1973, for example, to a recent year, we have to consider several factors. As shown in table 13–1, the demographics of the population have changed significantly. Over the sixteen-year period shown the number of families

TABLE 13–1
Changes in Population, Family Composition, and Income, 1973 and 1989
(in thousands)

	1973	1989	% Change 1973–1989
Number of families	73,166	101,663	38.9
Families with children	31,098	34,768	11.8
Married couples with children	24,798	24,378	-1.7
Single mothers with children	4,126	7,123	72.6
Nonelderly childless units	28,183	46,467	64.9
Elderly childless units	13,884	20,428	47.1
Number of persons in all families	207,525	245,846	18.5
Families with children	134,248	135,381	0.8
Married couples with children	108,976	99,471	-8.7
Single mothers with children	14,240	21,504	51.0
Nonelderly childless units	50,148	77,025	53.6
Elderly childless units	23,129	33,440	44.6

SOURCE: Congressional Budget Office tabulations of data from the March Current Population Survey, 1974 and 1990.

in the United States increased by about 40 percent. The number of families with children, however, increased by only 12 percent. All of the increase in families with children was in families headed by a female. The number of married couples with children declined by 400,000 families between 1973 and 1989. The number of elderly childless units increased by 47 percent.

While the number of family units increased by 40 percent, the population was increasing by only 19 percent. As a consequence, average family size declined by 16 percent from an average of 2.87 persons per family to 2.4 persons per family. Despite the decline in families consisting of married couples with children, more than 40 percent of the population lives in this type of family. Slightly more than 55 percent of the population resides in families with children.

Given these demographic changes and depending on the method of measuring income distribution, one can arrive at quite different conclusions. Table 13–2 demonstrates how different income distribution mea-

110

TABLE 13-2

ALTERNATIVE MEASURES OF FAMILY INCOME, BY INCOME QUINTILE
AND CHANGE OVER TIME, FOR ALL FAMILIES, 1973 AND 1989
(1989 dollars)

Pre-Tax Income, by Quintile	1973	1989	% Change 1973–1989
A. Mean family cash income, family-weighted			
Lowest	6,061	5,866	−3.2
Second	15,416	15,107	−2.0
Middle	25,909	25,823	−0.3
Fourth	37,946	40,374	6.4
Highest	66,364	77,716	17.1
Average	30,341	32,978	8.7
B. Adjusted family income, person-weighted[a]			
Lowest	0.90	0.86	−4.3
Second	1.94	2.09	7.7
Middle	2.82	3.27	16.0
Fourth	3.94	4.77	20.9
Highest	6.87	8.84	28.7
Average	3.29	3.97	20.4
C. Mean family income per capita, person-weighted[b]			
Lowest	2,795	2,822	1.0
Second	5,906	6.872	16.4
Middle	8,628	10,723	24.3
Fourth	12,386	16,058	29.6
Highest	23,875	32,237	35.0
Average	10,718	13,743	28.2

a. Adjusted family income is income divided by the poverty threshold.
b. Per capita income is family income divided by family size.
SOURCE: Congressional Budget Office tabulations of data from the March
Current Population Survey, 1974 and 1990.

sures illustrate the population's relative well-being at different income strata. Panels A, B, and C are based on the same census source, which uses the same concept of income and the same price inflator (the CPI–X1) to adjust 1973 dollars to 1989 dollars.

Panel A divides the entire population into quintiles, or one-fifths, on the basis of family cash income. "Family" includes single individuals living alone. In 1989 the income of the bottom quintile—the poorest one-fifth of all families—decreased 3 percent relative to the poorest one-fifth of families in 1973. The income of the middle one-fifth stayed about the same in 1989 compared with 1973, while income of the richest quintile of families gained more than 17 percent in real terms. In comparing well-being in this analysis, we assume that a family of six can live as cheaply as a family of one.

In panel C we make the reverse assumption. We assume that a family of six requires six times as much income as a family of one. This analysis takes family income and divides by the number of people in the family. Individuals are then sorted by per capita income, so that each quintile contains exactly 20 percent of the population.

The real percentage change in income at the bottom quintile shows a small increase of 1 percent between 1973 and 1989; the middle quintile shows a 24 percent increase in real income in this period; and the income of the highest quintile increased by 35 percent. These two panels paint a substantially different picture of what happened to income distribution in this country.

In assessing income distribution I use the family size adjustors implicit in the poverty guidelines. Although they could be improved, they are readily available and are preferable to the alternative assumptions used in panels A and C. Panel B takes family income and divides first by the poverty threshold which expresses income as a multiple of the poverty threshold. Families are sorted from low to high on the basis of this multiple, and 20 percent of the population is placed into each quintile. Under this measure of income distribution the income of the poorest quintile declined by 4 percent between 1973 and 1989, while the richest 20 percent of the population had real income gains of almost 30 percent.

Table 13–2 illustrates what happened to the income distribution for the entire population. Some equally important changes occurred among different demographic groups, as shown in table 13–3 constructed in the same manner as panel B in table 13–2. The population is divided into three groups—families with children, nonelderly child-

112

TABLE 13–3
AVERAGE FAMILY CASH INCOME AS A FRACTION OF POVERTY, 1973 AND 1989

Family Type and Quintile	1973	1989	% change 1973–1989
All families with children			
Lowest	0.88	0.74	−16.1
Second	1.88	1.87	−0.7
Middle	2.65	2.93	10.8
Fourth	3.54	4.14	16.9
Highest	5.73	7.20	25.6
Average	2.94	3.38	14.9
Nonelderly childless units			
Lowest	1.22	1.19	−1.8
Second	2.81	2.94	4.5
Middle	4.09	4.45	8.9
Fourth	5.49	6.29	14.5
Highest	8.95	10.94	22.3
Average	4.51	5.16	14.4
Elderly childless units			
Lowest	0.76	0.95	24.7
Second	1.34	1.73	28.6
Middle	1.97	2.64	34.1
Fourth	3.02	4.02	33.2
Highest	6.54	8.63	32.0
Average	2.73	3.59	31.8

NOTE: Average family cash income is adjusted family income. Figures are adjusted by family type. Quintiles are based on adjusted family cash income. Figures are weighted by persons.
SOURCE: Congressional Budget Office.

less families, and elderly families. Each quintile contains 20 percent of the population within that demographic group. Families with children in the poorest quintile experienced an income loss of 16 percent between 1973 and 1989. All quintiles among the elderly gained substantial amounts of real income. That is one of the primary reasons why Senator

Al Gore and Congressman Tom Downey proposed converting the personal exemption to a refundable tax credit for children under the age of eighteen.

Some of the income gains of the second, middle, and fourth quintiles are due to higher female earnings. If female earnings had remained constant in real terms between 1973 and 1989, the bottom four quintiles for married couples with children would have had real income losses. In reality, only the bottom quintile showed a small loss of 2 percent during this time period.

Table 13–4 expresses all these data in similar fashion. It shows what happened to family incomes by quintiles of the total population, ranked by family cash income in relationship to the poverty level. It uses a different Congressional Budget Office income model, one that has taken census data and merged them with Statistics of Income data. This eliminates the top-coding problem with census data, and the data set also contains enough observation at the top of the income distribution to allow the top quintile to be subdivided into smaller groups.

In this analysis, the bottom 40 percent of the population on average lost income in real terms between 1977 and 1989. In sharp contrast,

TABLE 13–4
PRE-TAX AND AFTER-TAX INCOME, INCOME SHARES, AND PERCENTAGE CHANGE, 1977–1989

	Percent Change in Pre-Tax Income 1977–1989	Percent Change in After-Tax Income 1977–1989	Pre-Tax Income Shares 1977	Pre-Tax Income Shares 1989	Federal Tax Shares 1977	Federal Tax Shares 1989
Lowest quintile	−8.8	−9.1	4.9	3.7	2.0	1.5
Second quintile	−1.3	−1.7	10.6	9.3	7.2	6.4
Middle quintile	4.2	4.5	15.7	14.6	13.4	12.5
Fourth quintile	9.1	9.1	22.5	21.4	21.6	20.8
Fifth quintile	29.0	32.0	46.6	51.8	55.7	58.6
Top 5 percent	46.6	55.5	20.6	26.0	27.7	30.4
Top 1 percent	77.1	101.7	8.7	13.0	13.6	15.4
Middle 60 percent	N.A.	N.A.	48.8	45.3	42.2	39.7

NOTE: N.A. = not applicable.
SOURCE: Congressional Budget Office.

the top 1 percent of the population had real after-tax income gains of 100 percent over this twelve-year period. As shown in column 4, the share of income going to the top 1 percent is equal to the total income of the bottom 40 million Americans. The income gains between 1977 and 1989 of the top 1 percent is more than the total income of the poorest 50 million Americans. These facts provide support and interest on Capitol Hill for some kind of middle-income tax relief bill—probably in the name of children.

The Gore-Downey bill redistributes about $20 billion of tax relief to families with children, with approximately 90 percent of the additional revenue coming from the top 1 percent of the population. That means that roughly 134 million Americans would receive a tax cut and about 15 million Americans would have a tax increase.

In summary, the tremendous growth in income among the richest Americans during the past decade and stagnating income growth among lower- and middle-income families mean that all tax policy proposals will be subjected to an income distribution test. Important institutional changes at both JCT and CBO will aid Congress in making that test. Analysis of tax policy proposals must include both revenue-loss and revenue-gain provisions, and those proposals that flunk the income-distribution test are not likely to pass Congress.

The budget rules and the goal of achieving long-term economic growth imply that tax policies must be budget-neutral. Every politician wishes to achieve greater economic growth and income gains for all Americans, particularly among low- and middle-income families. The question is, Which policy or combination of policies has the greatest probability of achieving that outcome? Investment in human capital, as compared with investments in real estate, plants or equipment, is more likely or just as likely to increase economic growth.

The Gore-Downey bill is likely to increase parental investments in children by increasing the income of the poorest families with children. It is undoubtedly true that investments in children increase with family income. By also increasing returns to work among low-wage workers, the bill increases the returns for parental investments in their own human capital. Thus, the Gore-Downey tax bill is as likely to increase economic growth as are proposals to increase national saving by expanding IRAs.

PART FIVE

Personal Tax Incentives, Fiscal Policy, and National Saving

14

Some Measurement and Policy Issues of National Saving and Investment

Robert Eisner

We should be concerned with national saving, we should be concerned with national saving correctly measured; and the national saving, correctly measured, is a far cry from what most people talk about. Aside from the corrections that we might make to conventional accounts, substantial extensions are to be made. Corrections are to be made to net foreign investment, for example, which are now just beginning to be effected, as we have new efforts, new estimates by the Bureau of Economic Analysis of the market value of international assets abroad. A large part of the apparent decline in national saving, a major part of it in the last decade, related to the presumed decline in net foreign investment, as it was measured.

There is good reason to believe that the apparent contributions of the capital consumption allowances to lower net saving are mismeasured. But more important even than these is the issue of what to do about the reported negative public saving, which we get from our federal deficit. We, almost alone of major countries, count all government expenditures as consumption, recognizing as public saving only those rare shortfalls of government expenditures against taxes extracted from the public.

With the encouragement of Michael Boskin, we are now moving toward the UN system of accounts, and will, at least in our national income accounting, be including government investment expenditures as part of investment. That will make a big difference in our measure of national saving.

Another big difference would come from recognizing the huge investment by households in durable goods. We count the purchase of a car by a household as personal consumption, by government as government consumption. If Avis happens to buy the car and we (or the government) rent it from Avis, it counts as investment.

A huge amount of what should be national saving is in intangible capital, in human capital, a great deal of which is furnished by government. It is an essential in any meaningful consideration of national saving.

Effects of Tax Incentives

Some years ago, after simulating the effects of tax incentives on investment and major econometric models, Robert Chirinko and I concluded that to proceed with such incentives "on the assumption that they will have commensurate effects in increasing investment must . . . rest essentially on faith. Faith is indeed sometimes rewarded. But for our part, in this instance, we remain agnostic."[1] Our results suggested, indeed, that the tax "incentives," if uncompensated by other tax increases, would lose considerably more in tax revenues—and increase "the deficit" more than they would increase investment.

I have even less reason to be sanguine about tax incentives focused on saving. They seem generally designed more to give tax relief to marginal voters than to affect the marginal propensity to save. In generally putting upper bounds on the amounts eligible for tax subsidies, presumably for reasons of equity and to curb tax losses to the Treasury, most of the proposals invite shifting portfolios of already accumulated savings rather than increases in the new flow.

I should confess that if I thought the various schemes were efficient and effective in bringing on more saving, I would be even more against them. I see no reason for Big Brother to influence his inferior siblings— or subjects—to save more than they are inclined to save on their own. It may be argued that government is already discouraging saving and these proposals are designed only to redress the balance. The current bias, I suggest, goes more the other way. Most saving is accomplished in the form of unrealized and untaxed capital gains and in untaxed accumulation of pension funds. Tax deductibility of swollen nominal interest costs has proved a further stimulus to investment and saving as taxable enterprises have taken the deductions while the receipts have gone disproportionately to those who have not paid taxes on them.

It must be recalled further that more saving can be accomplished only to the extent it is embodied in more investment—domestic or foreign. On the domestic side the increased investment induced by increasing the propensity to save would be what is induced by a lower cost of capital and hence with lower marginal product. Bringing on investment with a low—even negative—marginal product is not the way to increase productivity or growth.

On the foreign side more saving may well increase net investment by reducing the current account deficit as consumption of foreign goods declines—along with the consumption of domestic goods. The latter reduction is more likely to trigger a recession than to increase domestic investment or the total of national saving.

Much discussion of tax incentives for saving and investment is improperly limited to microeconomic analysis. Proposals to increase desired saving, in particular, raise fundamental issues of how their effects will work their way through the economy as a whole and with what consequences. The saving-investment identity shown in table 14–1 reminds us that increased incentives, desires, or propensities to save in the aggregate can be realized only by increasing aggregate investment.

Individuals or households undertake to save more to the extent that they undertake to earn more income that they do not spend. If, as "supply-siders" argue, an incentive does induce us to earn more and we do not consume all of the added earnings, then we save more. But the various incentives are more likely, if they are effective, chiefly to induce people to consume less. To take the accounting identity that saving equals income minus consumption (and government expenditures) as evidence that reducing consumption must raise national saving should be recognized, on even the slightest reflection, as patently absurd. It is startlingly akin to the assumption, more than half a century ago, that saving and investment would be increased if we all undertook voluntarily to save more by consuming less. Perhaps. But that is exactly the proposition to be proved, or supported by empirical evidence, not assumed.[2]

My usual quip is to ask if our decision to "consume" less by not buying that new Chrysler is going to induce Mr. Iacocca to invest more—or less. I may get a retort that I am not looking at the long run. In the long run, others may say, if we all try to save more, we will have more saving. The long run is a succession of short runs. It may well be that if we follow policies that perpetually, period after period, give us higher average unemployment, we will find that our efforts to save more result in less investment and less saving.

I can offer a bit of evidence from an economy in which 7 percent

TABLE 14–1
NET SAVING AND INVESTMENT ACCOUNT, 1990
(billions of dollars)

Gross private domestic investment	741.0	Personal income	4,645.5
Less capital consumption allowances with capital consumption adjustment	575.6	Less personal tax and nontax payments	699.4
Net private domestic investment	165.4	Less personal outlays	3,766.0
Net foreign investment	−85.5	personal consumption expenditures	3,657.3
		interest paid by consumers to business	107.8
		personal transfer payments to foreigners	0.9
		Personal saving	180.1
		Undistributed corporate profits with inventory valuation and capital consumption adjustment	32.2
		Government surplus or deficit (−), national income and product accounts	−130.6
		federal	−166.0
		state and local	35.4
		Net saving	81.7
		Statistical discrepancy	−1.7
Net investment	80.0	Net saving and statistical discrepancy	80.0

SOURCE: Adapted from *Survey of Current Business*, May 1991, tables 1.1, 1.9, 2.1, and 5.1, pp. 8, 10, 12, and 15.

unemployment is, sadly, closer to the norm than the 5 percent or 4 percent that some of us have looked to as full employment. In that economy—our own—that old warhorse for reducing consumption—reducing the budget deficit—has apparently operated not to increase national saving but to reduce it. I have, using annual time-series data, regressed the conventional national saving rate on the previous real, or inflation-adjusted, structural federal deficit along with changes in the real monetary base and real exchange rate over the years 1972 to 1990 and found those deficits associated positively with subsequent saving rates. In fact (with a regression coefficient of .905 and standard error of .366 in a first-difference formulation), each percentage point of deficit, expressed as a ratio of GNP, was associated with nine-tenths of a percentage point more of subsequent saving. Increases in the real monetary base and declines in the real exchange rate were also clearly and significantly related to subsequent increases in national saving. They apparently stimulated the economy to more output, domestic investment, and net exports, just as our theories of aggregate demand, when the economy is not at its full potential, would suggest. Consistent with the saving-investment identity, larger, inflation-adjusted, structural deficits have been followed by less net foreign investment but more domestic investment. The balance, even for our conventional measures of saving and investment, has hence been positive; gross investment, like saving, has been positively associated with prior real, structural deficits. These findings are all supported by results of vector autoregressions.[3]

Productive Public Investment

But as noted, the conventional measure of national saving—gross private domestic investment plus net foreign investment—is far from a relevant one. Debates are finally arising as to whether at least some public investment may not be more productive than private investment. Although the American Enterprise Institute sponsored a conference on that, the possibility was largely ignored until recently. Surely, economically relevant saving should comprise all acquisition of tangible goods, whether by business, nonprofit institutions, households, or government. And it should comprise as well much intangible investment, in health, in research and development, and in education. Indeed, one of the proposals we have been considering offers explicit incentives to private expenditures for education. But the usual proposals to reduce budget deficits would either cut government expenditures, including government investment expenditures, or raise taxes to reduce private consumption, including private investment in durable goods.

Bearing directly on all this, I can also report the results of regressions relating to investment in consumer durables and the measures of investment that include them—private domestic tangible and private tangible investment—and those for broader measures of national saving corresponding to the more comprehensive measures of investment. As might be expected, they show budget deficits, with all they imply for consumption and government expenditures, even more positively related to those broader, more relevant measures of national saving.

If you reduce the budget deficit by holding down government expenditures on roads, bridges, and infrastructure generally, on education and on research, are you really adding to national saving? My regressions certainly indicate not.

What is my conclusion from all this? The best way to increase national saving is first to ensure that we have a prosperous economy. This would be helped by relaxed and stimulative monetary policies and by avoidance of, not accentuation of, fiscal austerity. It would also be helped by assuring adequate rates of productive public investment in our nation's future. I would leave private saving in a prosperous economy to the joint decisions of households and enterprises in a free market.

An important, perhaps most important, component of national saving, properly measured, involves investment in intangible capital and public investment. There is good reason to suspect that this investment, little affected by market considerations, is inadequate. It is here that we should look for solution of our real problems.

15

Is There a Problem with Tax Policy and National Saving?

William A. Niskanen

There are three general points with this issue. First, there is reason to believe that our saving rate is too low. That is not indicated, however, by the level of the saving rate but by the fact that we have, at some margins, a double taxation of deferred consumption. Second, it is not clear that this problem is significantly worse now than it was in 1979, regardless of what the numbers in the national income accounts show. And third, the major fiscal effects on the saving rate are much larger than any conceivable effects that might be attributable to IRAs, either in the past or in the future.

Low Saving Rate?

Let me expand on these three points. First, there is a general reason why the saving rate is too low. At the margin, outside the limited shelter provided for social security, pensions, and the annuity value of housing, deferred consumption is subject to double taxation. That is the case in any income tax system that taxes both the income saved and the income from saving. This increases the relative price of deferred consumption by the amount of the marginal tax rate on income and should be expected to increase current consumption and to reduce current saving.

Some types of savings that are exempt from taxation when the contribution was made—such as the employer's share of social security payroll taxes, pension contributions, and the IRAs of the early 1980s— are essentially taxed only once, at the point where they are realized as income available for consumption during retirement years. At the

125

margin, however—for savings outside these provisions and in excess of the amounts they provide for—we have a double taxation of deferred consumption. For that reason, there should be a presumption that the individual saving rate, whatever the numbers show, is too low.

Decrease in Saving?

Second, it is not obvious that the general problem of saving is worse than it was in 1979 even though the national income account numbers look rather disturbing. Note what the numbers show for changes between 1979 and 1989 in the gross savings as a percentage of GNP. (See chapter 6, by Rudolph Penner, for a graphical summary of those numbers.)

The personal saving rate fell from 4.7 to 3.3 percent of GNP, a reduction of 1.4 percentage points. Gross business saving fell from 13.1 to 11.7 percent of GNP, a reduction also of 1.4 percentage points. The government saving rate fell from plus 0.5 percent of GNP (the combined federal, state, and local surplus or deficit, as conventionally measured) to a minus 1.7, a change of minus 2.2 percentage points. The gross saving rate, thus, fell from 18.3 to 13.3 percent of GNP, a reduction of 5 percentage points, nearly half of which was accounted for by the change in the government saving rate and roughly a quarter each by changes in the personal saving rate and in the business saving rate, respectively.

Let us look at these three components of the change to see whether there is reason to believe that conditions have, in some sense, really deteriorated. The personal saving rate from the national income accounts is a little misleading because it reflects only savings out of current income and does not reflect changes in the value of assets that people held at the beginning of the period.

The Federal Reserve System's set of accounts, however, reveals a different story. In a comparison of both the national income numbers on personal saving and the Federal Reserve System numbers in personal saving, in this case as a percentage of disposable income, the national income numbers show a drop from 6.8 percent of disposable personal income in 1979 to 4.6 percent in 1989—a decline of 2.2 percentage points of disposable personal income—whereas the Federal Reserve System numbers show an increase from 11.8 to 11.9 percent of disposable income over this same decade. In terms of the savings measured as savings out of current income plus the increase in the value of the assets held at the beginning of the period, the average household saving rate was slightly higher in 1989 than at the beginning of the decade. In addition, based upon my criterion of reducing the double taxation of deferred consumption, the lower marginal tax rates at the end of this period than at the beginning of this period reduced the tax wedge on deferred consumption.

The contribution to the reduction in the gross saving rate by business, again 1.4 percentage points of GNP over this decade, was largely attributable to the decline of 19 percent in the real price of business fixed investment goods during this period. As a consequence, the business sector was able to maintain a roughly average gross real investment rate, despite the substantial reduction in their gross saving rate.

Nearly half of the reduction in the gross saving rate, then, is attributable to the change in the government's saving position, a reduction of 2.2 percentage points of GNP. That turns out to be roughly equal to the increase in the share of GNP going to defense over that same period.

The key issue here is whether we really bought significant capital with that big defense buildup, capital that will generate a stream of returns to people in the 1990s and subsequently that will justify the deficit-financed defense buildup. That issue is not easily resolved, even by the most careful analysis. But what should be recognized is that the major increase in government spending in the 1980s—for defense—was of roughly the same magnitude as the reduction in the saving rate attributable to government. We should consider carefully whether we actually added assets of any meaningful value by making these additional federal government expenditures.

For each of the three components of gross savings—personal savings, business savings, and government savings—the numbers between 1979 and 1989 look disturbing. But in terms of what happened in each of these individual sectors, it is not at all clear that savings behavior was significantly less optimal at the end than at the beginning of the period.

Major Fiscal Effects

My third point is that the major fiscal effects on saving rates are not those that result from detailed tax provisions such as IRAs or similar plans; they are instead effects that operate through real interest rates, through the real value of wealth—basically through macro phenomena rather than through the detailed provisions of the IRAs. With respect to

127

the IRAs, this is one case where, when the evidence is confusing, we should trust our theory. The theory is fairly straightforward. For those who made the full allowed IRA contribution, there is no substitution effect, but there is a wealth effect that should increase consumption and reduce savings. These people received an inframarginal lump-sum tax reduction.

That lump-sum tax reduction should be expected to increase consumption and reduce saving by those people who make the full IRA contribution. There is no substitution effect at the margin for those who make the full contribution. So for those who make the full contribution, there is reason to believe that IRAs would increase their consumption and reduce their saving. Most of the contributions into the IRAs over that period, from 1982 to 1986 or so, were by people who made their full contribution.

For those people who did not make the full contribution, there was a positive substitution effect because the price of future consumption is reduced. Whether the IRAs contributed at all to increased personal saving—let alone what they did to the deficit—depends on whether the impact on total savings of the wealth effect for those who made the full contribution was larger or smaller than the impact of the substitution effect for those who made less than the full contribution.

There is a plausible reason to believe that the IRAs might have reduced personal savings. National savings would be reduced, in addition, by the reduction in federal revenues and the resulting increase in the federal deficit.

The major effects on saving during the 1980s were macro effects, such as whatever drove the real interest rates up so sharply through 1985 and then drove them down later in the decade. The primary fiscal condition that contributed to the increase and subsequent decline in real interest rates was not the deficit but instead the preferred tax treatment of business investment in the Economic Recovery Tax Act of 1981 and the dramatic subsequent change in the tax treatment of business investment in the Tax Reform Act of 1986.

The other condition was whatever led to the dramatic increase in the real value of financial assets. To the extent that personal consumption is a function of both income and wealth, an increase in wealth will reduce saving out of current income.

So for the same level of income, if wealth goes up, one should increase consumption and reduce saving out of current income. A significant part of the reduction in personal saving during the 1980s— as measured in the national income accounts—was a consequence of

128

the increase in the value of household assets or personal wealth. The household balance sheet looked better at the end than at the beginning of the decade, even though saving out of current income fell.

In summary, the focus on saving is a legitimate issue. Whether the low saving rate is legitimately a matter of concern, however, cannot be determined by whether the numbers look low or high. The question instead is whether the conditions influencing saving decisions lead the individual actors in each sector to make efficient decisions on the average or not. You cannot tell that from the numbers; you have to look at the conditions faced by the decision makers in each of these sectors.

There is reason to worry about the low saving rate. It is not clear, however, that we are in a significantly worse situation in 1989 or 1990 or 1991 than we were in 1979. And finally, the focus on IRAs or IRA-like accounts is a diversion of attention. Changing the tax provisions for IRAs, with the hope that this change would increase the national saving rate, is much like spitting in the ocean.

16

Fiscal Policy and the Economy

Robert D. Reischauer

The legislative options should be placed in the broader context of public policy. We would not be debating the desirability of enacting legislation to expand IRAs, to cut payroll taxes, or to provide refundable credits for children but for the fact that the growth of productivity, real wages and, ultimately, living standards slowed markedly after 1973. These developments have had a number of troubling consequences, four of which are worth noting.

First, the slowdown has left a sizable portion of the population, primarily those whose educational attainments are limited, with stagnant or even falling real incomes. It is no accident that the homeless and the underclass have emerged during the past two decades.

Second, the sluggish growth in living standards has generated an unhealthy obsession with issues of distribution. When the national pie fails to grow at an acceptable pace, every group becomes much more concerned about the relative size of its slice. Issues like affirmative action admissions to colleges, hiring preferences, and the distributional consequences of changes in cigarette and alcohol taxes become both more important and more divisive.

Third, the slow rise in living standards has made the public less willing to fund government programs, both existing and new. In this context, the tax revolts of the past decade and a half may be interpreted as an effort to improve or to maintain living standards in the face of stagnant or falling real wages. This reaction has undermined our ability to deal with those problems that have traditionally been handled collectively, such as the crumbling infrastructure and the inadequacies of our educational and training systems.

Finally, the anemic growth in living standards has eroded America's image abroad, and with it our ability to project the values we think are important. American influence is diminishing as other economies show themselves to be more dynamic and better able to minimize the hardships associated with an efficient market economy. Our capacity to be a stabilizing influence in the world has decreased at a time when the order imposed by the cold war is giving way to drift and chaos.

Responses to the Problem

Policy makers have responded to the slowdown in the growth of living standards with two different types of tax proposals. Both represent second-best solutions to the problems that face the nation.

Proposals to Encourage Personal Saving. The first approach encompasses the various proposals to encourage personal saving through the tax system. If successful, such policies would increase national saving and investment, thereby improving productivity, economic growth, and future living standards. But how sure are we that these policies will succeed? And what will be the consequences if they do not?

There are a number of reasons to be skeptical about the effectiveness of tax policies directed at encouraging private saving. First, a substantial body of evidence suggests that personal saving is relatively insensitive to changes in the rate of return since the income and substitution effects roughly offset each other. Second, tax incentives will increase the deficit, exacerbating government dissaving. If national saving is to increase, the hoped-for increase in personal saving must exceed the federal government's revenue loss. The Budget Enforcement Act of 1990 has provided some short-term safeguards on this front by requiring that any policy-induced revenue loss be offset by reductions in entitlement spending or by increases in other taxes. But this restriction ends in 1995, and back-loaded plans can be designed to circumvent the restriction.

A third reason for skepticism about the potential of these proposals relates to the various eligibility limits they all have established to make them more politically acceptable. These limits—designed to mitigate their distributional and revenue-loss effects—eliminate the marginal incentives for high-income savers, without whose participation the total impact on saving is likely to be small.

Reducing the Federal Deficit As a Better Alternative. Given our huge federal deficits, and the uncertainty as to whether tax incentives can stimulate private saving, one must ask whether there are alternatives. Are there more certain ways in increasing national saving and investment? The answer to this question is yes.

One response would be to reduce the federal deficit by cutting spending or raising taxes. The deficit, which represents government dissaving, will be at historically high levels over the next few years despite the enactment of a significant package of deficit reduction measures last year. In fiscal year 1991 the deficit will be close to $270 billion, and in fiscal year 1992 it will be more than $350 billion. These figures include the ballooning costs of deposit insurance, which for various reasons should be left out when we decide how much collective concern to express over the economic damage inflicted by megadeficits. But even when deposit insurance spending is removed, the adjusted deficits through 1994 will represent a higher fraction of GNP than they did in 1988, 1989, or 1990. In short, we have a long way to go before the deficit comes down to acceptable levels. If deficit reduction is pursued as a preferable alternative for spurring growth, then spending cuts should not be made in programs directed at productive public investment, and tax increases should be skewed toward reducing consumption.

Even without a further attack on the deficit, economic growth and future living standards could be stimulated if we were willing to reorient federal spending significantly in the direction of infrastructure, research and development, and education-training or if we would agree to rearrange taxes so as to put a heavier burden on consumption. A 1992 study by the Congressional Budget Office estimates that future output would increase by a modest 0.8 percent if we lowered income tax rates by one-quarter and replaced the lost revenue with a 6 percent broad-based value-added tax.

Another way to attack the problem of slow growth in living standards—an alternative to providing tax incentives for personal saving—would be to use the tax system to encourage investment. This approach might be a more effective way to expand the capital stock because it could tap into the pool of foreign saving and could be targeted on the types of capital spending that are thought to be most important to economic growth. Residential housing and commercial office space, for example, could be excluded from the benefits. Following the recent work of Bradford De Long and Lawrence Summers on the impact of various types of investment on economic growth, the incentives could be limited to investment in equipment.[1]

The reason why politicians find tax incentives for saving the most

132

appealing approach to boosting future living standards is no mystery. Such incentives seem to offer some gain for everybody without inflicting pain on any particular group. From the politician's vantage point, such schemes are preferable to "some gain with no pain at all" because they offer a benefit—a tax break—to those who voluntarily save.

The other options for increasing national saving or investment involve less pleasant choices. The deficit can be reduced only by cutting particular spending programs or by raising some individual's or group's taxes. Neither of these possibilities has much political appeal when the expected benefits from higher living standards are distant, diffused in an unknown way among many citizens, and only modest in size. Rearranging the composition of spending or taxes produces losers as well as winners, while encouraging investment with tax breaks for business generates fewer direct winners, and few who vote.

There are reasons, other than political acceptability, to support tax incentives for saving. Such incentives could represent an important, and much needed, signal that saving and frugality are not un-American. In our headlong pursuit of life, liberty, and happiness, Americans have put a premium on instant gratification and consumption. We have created a multibillion dollar advertising industry devoted to convincing us that we must have at least one of everything that is available and that people will judge us by what we wear, eat, and drive. We have developed a system that extends credit for consumption to almost anyone who has any prospect of future earnings. Some antidote to this is needed, and if it does not come from the government, it will not come from anywhere.

Proposals to Redistribute Income. The second approach to the slowdown in the growth of living standards encompasses various tax proposals designed to increase the aftertax incomes of those who have not benefited much from the economic growth of the past two decades. Included in this group of policies are the proposals to help workers by reducing the payroll tax, the proposals to help families with children by substituting a partially refundable tax credit of $800 to $1,000 for the personal exemption for children, the proposals to double the personal exemption, and the proposals to expand the earned income tax credit—particularly for those with more than two children.

For the most part, these proposals are designed to ameliorate the immediate consequences of the slowdown in the growth of incomes, not to deal with the underlying causes of the problem. In other words, they seek to reslice the existing pie rather than to bake a larger one. To the extent that these proposals would increase the deficit, they could even

133

end up reducing the size of the pie for future generations. The CBO has estimated, for example, that if the social security system were returned to a pay-as-you-go regime, which would involve cutting employee and employer taxes each by about one percentage point, and if there were no offsetting changes in the rest of the budget, real GNP in the period 1997 to 2016 would be reduced by roughly $150 per capita a year from what it would otherwise be.[2]

These proposals are motivated largely by considerations of equity, which, being in the eye of the beholder, cannot be evaluated using analytic tools. Nevertheless, one can ask whether those who are proposing tax cuts for families or tax cuts for the middle class really believe that if $25 billion or $50 billion a year were available to devote to children or middle-class workers, it would be best spent increasing current disposable incomes.

Most of the increase in disposable income would be spent on current consumption. But few would argue that private consumption is too low except among the poorest Americans, few of whom would benefit significantly from any of these proposals. The research of Christopher Jenks and others suggests that there has been a steady increase in the material possessions and lifestyles of even fairly low-income Americans. One can point to widespread ownership of many items that three decades ago were regarded as luxuries or did not exist—color televisions, dishwashers, air conditioning, automobiles, audio equipment, and the like. Luxuries that were once largely enjoyed only by the affluent, such as restaurant meals, air travel, home screenings of movies (videocassette recorders), and vacations abroad, have become readily available to the broad middle class.

To be sure, some may consider that the distribution of consumption is obscene when some households have four cars, six telephones and three color televisions while others have only one of each. And certainly some people lack even the basics of life in a civilized society, namely, adequate food, shelter, and medical care. A recent study of hunger among American children brought this out vividly.[3] But the tax-cut proposals being put forward today would have only a marginal impact on the inadequate consumption levels of the poor. A more effective way of dealing with this problem would be a liberalization of the food stamp program, an increase in benefits to families with dependent children, or an expansion of Medicaid.

Rather than expanding private consumption, many people would argue that what the children and workers of America need most is better preschool education, better elementary and secondary schools, safer and less violent neighborhoods, a better system of job training and retraining, and more productive jobs. Substantial moves in these directions, however, have been stymied for the past decade and will be even more difficult. The discretionary spending caps established by the Budget Enforcement Act of 1990 require that if more resources are devoted to Head Start, Chapter I educational assistance, the Job Corps, productive public sector physical investments or enhanced R&D, less must be provided for some other discretionary programs.

Conclusion

Let me reiterate my basic message, which is that if the nation wants to address the underlying causes of the slowdown in productivity growth and the resulting stagnation of living standards among many, the tax policies that have generally been discussed are no more than second-best solutions. Deficit reduction remains the most effective, even if politically unpalatable, response to the problem.

17

What to Do about the Collapse of National Saving

Charles L. Schultze

I want to state and to present briefly evidence for several propositions about the U.S. national saving rate and policies to affect it. To begin, we must agree upon a definition of national savings. There are four alternative concepts (see figure 17–1): gross and net savings, with or without public investment. Measured as a share of national output (NNP), the saving rate under all four definitions fell sharply: between three and one-half and six and one-half percentage points over the past decade. For this chapter, I use the net measure without public investment, for dealing with issues of long-term national growth, but the story would basically not change if one of the other definitions were employed.

Some have argued that the national income and product accounts (NIPA) definition for national savings is flawed. In particular, they argue, the large real estate and stock market capital gains of the 1980s are not included in the NIPA measures that form the basis for the estimates in figure 17–1. It would take a great deal of time to address this point properly. At this stage let me simply note that while capital gains are an important element in an analysis of the determinants of private saving, the NIPA measure, which excludes capital gains, is the proper measure to answer the question of what proportion of current national output is being devoted each year to adding to the nation's stock of productive assets. To include in this measure changes in the market valuation of private wealth would give an entirely misleading estimate. Japan, for example, with its incredible runup in real estate prices before 1990, would be deemed many times wealthier than the United States; a decrease in the number of taxis in New York City by raising cab

FIGURE 17–1

ALTERNATIVE DEFINITIONS OF U.S. NATIONAL SAVING, 1951–1990

Percentage of GNP or NNP[a]

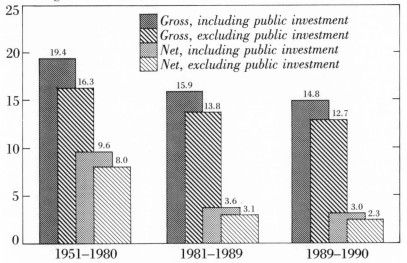

a. Gross and net saving as shares of gross and net national product, respectively.
SOURCE: Author's calculations based on national income accounts data (prior to 1991 revisions) and Department of Commerce (BEA) estimates of public (nonmilitary) investment and depreciation.

medallion prices would increase national wealth; and a population boom, by driving up land values, would also raise national wealth. A little reflection will show that changes in the market valuation of private wealth do not belong in the definition of national saving used to measure the contribution to future economic growth that comes from refraining from consumption. In short, the NIPA measures used in figure 17–1 are the appropriate ones; the national saving rate has indeed fallen dramatically.

What are the prospects for the national saving rate in the medium-term future (the remainder of 1990s)? In figure 17–2, the 1996 projected net national saving rate as a percentage of NNP, excluding public investment, is based upon two assumptions:

1. The private saving rate remains at current levels (1989–1990), and the middle-of-the-road economic forecast of the Congressional Budget Office is realized.
2. The budget agreement holds, and no further deficit reduction is undertaken. The result is a federal deficit in the neighborhood of $150 billion by 1996.

137

According to this projection, the national saving rate will recover slightly to between 3 ½ and 4 percent of NNP by 1996.

A National Saving Target

How serious is the prospect of a national saving rate that low, approximately one-half of what it was in the three decades before the 1980s? If the situation is viewed from business-as-usual standpoint, the investment opportunities and requirements of the current era are lower than in earlier periods; in a sense we do not "need" as much investment. Labor force growth will be much lower than in prior decades. As a result, less capital formation is needed to equip the growing labor force with the average amount of capital. In addition, the rate of technical progress has diminished, and growth in the amount of capital per worker, consistent with a steady profit rate, is therefore lower. Maintaining the current rate of labor productivity growth would require an estimated net investment of about 4½ percent of NNP, compared with roughly 7½ percent in the earlier (1951–1980) period. But the projected rate of national saving, 3.8 percent of NNP, indicated in figure 17–2 is not enough, on its own, to sustain even that unambitious rate of investment. If the national saving rate does not rise, the current rate of domestic investment and productivity growth will have to fall even further, or alternatively the nation will have to continue to finance some of that minimal level of investment from abroad by diverting a fraction of its productivity payoff to the payment of overseas debt service.

In fact, the situation is worse than this. The business-as-usual approach to evaluating the sufficiency of national saving, as spelled out above, fails to take into account the massive changes in the nation's demographic profile that will face the United States in the early years of the next century. I refer to the large increase in the ratio of retirees to workers that will begin in the years after 2010—less than two decades from now.

Recognizing, at least in part, the desirability of moderating the potential burden on the next working generation, the executive branch and Congress in 1978 and again in 1983 raised the payroll tax schedule, reduced further benefits under the social security program, and began building up a surplus in the Social Security Trust Fund and other retirement programs of the federal government. But the simple accumulation of a financial surplus in various public retirement programs will not by itself enable the current generation to make provision in advance for its own retirement and reduce the burden on the next generation.

138

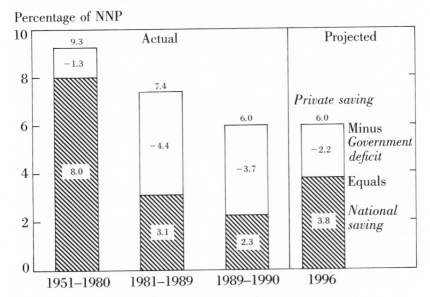

FIGURE 17–2
U.S. NATIONAL SAVING RATE, 1951–1996
(net, excluding public investment)

SOURCE: Government budget deficits in 1989–1990 and 1996 exclude deposit insurance.

The only way for this generation to pay for its own retirement is for the nation now to adopt policies under which the surpluses in the public retirement accounts are used to increase national saving over and above the business-as-usual amount. The additional national saving would then be available to invest in productive assets so that when the bulge of retirees does occur, their consumption will come out of a higher national income, thereby avoiding the additional burden on the working generation of the time.

A Projected Saving Rate with Unchanged Economic Policies

By the middle of the 1990s the annual surpluses in the federal government's retirement accounts will amount to about 3 percent of national income. If that 3 percent is added to the 4½ percent business-as-usual saving rate, we get a conservative national saving target of 7½ percent. This 7.5 percent target is three to four percentage points above the saving rate that will occur if private saving remains at its current level

139

FIGURE 17-3
PRIVATE SAVING AND DEMOGRAPHICS, 1956–1996

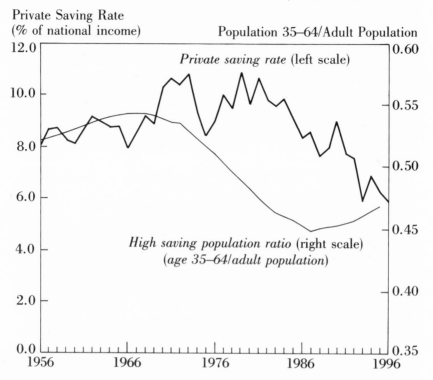

NOTE: The private saving rate includes state and local pension fund surplus for own employees.
SOURCE: Author.

and federal budget policy remains unchanged.

What is the prospect that private saving will return to its earlier level—approximately 9 percent of national income—and thereby bail us out? One popular argument is the supposed effect of the demographic changes that will affect the United States during the next forty to fifty years. According to this argument, the savings decline of the 1980s was caused by a large increase in the number of the young-adult, low-saving, baby boomers in the population. As they age, and the fraction of high-saving age group rises, private saving will be restored. Unfortunately, this assumption does not fit the facts. First, it is apparent in figure 17–3 that the timing is way off; the fraction of supposed high-savers started down a decade before the fall in private saving began. The high-

140

saving age group as a proportion of the rest of the U.S. population started up in the early to mid-1980s, when saving decline was greatest. More important, a recent analysis of changes in saving by age group shows that the decline in saving occurred within each age group and was not caused by a shift of population away from the high-saving age groups. That analysis calculated what the change in the total personal saving rate would have been, given the change that occurred in the saving rates of each age group over the recent past, but with the population age mixture held constant (see table 17–1). The drop in savings would have been almost as great as actually occurred; this change in the age mixture played little role.

In summary, demographic shifts did not cause the fall in private saving, and their projected reversal is unlikely to raise the total private saving rate. The cause of the decline in private saving remains something of a mystery, and no one should be confident of projecting the future. But for planning purposes, it would be prudent to assume that we cannot await rescue by a fortuitous rise in the private saving rate.

What, then, is the likelihood that judicious application of tax incentives could bring about a major rise in private saving? My evaluation of the evidence is pessimistic. First, since economic theory itself

TABLE 17–1
DEMOGRAPHIC MIXTURE AND THE CHANGE IN THE PERSONAL SAVING RATE, 1962–1985
(percent of personal income)

	Actual Saving Rate	Rate with Age Mixture Constant	Rate with Age and Income Mixture Constant
Survey of Consumer Finances			
1962–1963	14.0	14.0	14.0
1983–1986	9.5	10.3	10.2
Consumer Expenditure Survey			
1972–1973	15.1	15.1	15.1
1982–1985	10.8	11.1	11.0
Mean change	−4.4	−3.8	−4.1

Source: Calculated from data in Barry Bosworth, Gary Burtless, and John Sabelhaus, "The Decline in Saving: Some Microeconomic Evidence," Brookings Paper on Economic Activity, no. 1 (1991), p. 202.

cannot even tell us in what direction saving will change in response to an alteration in the rate of return, we have to rely on evidence from empirical studies. Not the unanimity but the bulk of the empirical evidence on the efficacy of changes in rates of return to alter saving behavior is negative. That evidence is well summed up by Rudiger Dornbusch and Stanley Fischer in the latest edition of their macroeconomics text: "Typically, research suggests the effects are small and certainly hard to find."

Second, the gross evidence during the 1980s flies squarely in the face of the view that savings is highly sensitive to changes in the rate of return. Real interest rates were at historically high levels, marginal tax rates were sharply cut, and individual retirement accounts (IRAs) were introduced. Yet private saving fell. To sustain the belief that increases in aftertax rates of return can significantly raise private saving, one would have to believe that faced with pre-1980 real rates of return, discretionary saving in the 1980s would for some reason have turned negative.

Third, my reading of the controversy on the substitutability of IRAs for other saving is that the William G. Gale–John Karl Scholz conclusions—that IRAs have principally substituted for other saving—is much more convincing than the Steven Venti–David Wise and Daniel Feenberg–Jonathan Skinner findings to the contrary.

On theoretical grounds the Venti–Wise assumption that IRAs should be treated as a separate new final good in the utility function, rather than a means for maximizing the expected utility from consumption, is an ad hoc and an unwarranted one, which may well bias their empirical results in the direction of low substitutability. Gale and Scholz avoid that assumption. Since the distinct possibility exists that the high-savers in the population are particularly likely to take advantage of IRAs, the Venti-Wise assumption of homogeneity of behavior may well be biasing upward their measures of the effect of IRAs on total saving. While not without problems, the Gale-Scholz approach avoids that dangerous assumption.

In sum, for all practical purposes, any serious effort to raise the national saving rate will have to depend heavily on reducing the federal budget deficit, not on increasing private savings. Indeed, to reach the 7½ percent target for the national saving rate I proposed earlier, the United States will have to go further and convert that deficit into a surplus. In turn, there is no way that can be accomplished without a sizable tax increase.

18

How to Get
Real People to Save

Richard H. Thaler

In social science, as well as in Washington, D.C., saving is considered the proper domain of economists, and no one else. This is unfortunate because economic theory provides less guidance than we might have hoped.

Lessons from Economic Theory

Suppose we have decided that we want to design a saving policy. (Whether we should have a savings policy is not an issue I will address.) What can we learn from economic theory that might be of some help? The relevant economic theory here is the life-cycle theory of saving originated by Franco Modigliani and the similar permanent income hypothesis suggested by Milton Friedman. One can hardly ask for more venerable theories or more distinguished authors. What do these theories tell us? The theories essentially provide a delineation of which variables should matter and which should not. That is, the theories indicate whether a change in a particular component of a saving policy should have any effect on savings.

Which policy variables matter? The most important policy variable is the aftertax rate of return to savings. If policy makers change the aftertax interest rate savers face, economic theory tells us that savers react. There is, however, one problem. The theory does not tell us in which direction savers will change their behavior. An income effect and a substitution effect go in opposite directions, and theory alone does not tell us which effect dominates. Empirical estimates do not help much

143

here either. Most of the empirical estimates of the effect of changes in the interest rate on personal saving find a negligible effect. This could mean that the income effect and substitution effect cancel, or it could be that savers are oblivious to interest rates. It is hard to say. The only other important variables in the life-cycle theory are age and wealth, and while making people younger and wealthier would solve many problems, these variables are not as yet feasible policy instruments. The bottom line is that the variables identified by the theory as important are not much help to policy makers.

What about the variables that the theory suggests should not matter? The long list of such variables includes anything that does not change age, wealth, or the rate of return. An example of such a variable is the source of income. Consider an individual whose wealth increases by $10,000. The theory predicts that the proportion of the $10,000 saved is the same regardless of whether the money was obtained by winning a lottery, making a good stock pick, or enjoying an increase in home equity. Even the news that the individual will receive an inheritance in eight years with a present value of $10,000 should, according to the theory, have the same effect on saving as any of the other windfalls. In every case the individual should save the annuity value of the windfall, that is, spread out the consumption of the windfall over his entire lifetime. In fact, the theory goes further. The proportion of the windfall that will be spent in the first year is not only independent of the source of the windfall but also independent of its magnitude. The equivalence of these various windfalls is a powerful prediction of the theory, but one that turns out to be wrong. Both the size and the source of windfall gains influence the proportion saved. I will say more about this later.

Similarly, the theory tells us that the timing of income flows does not matter. A lottery prize of $100,000 will be spent the same way, regardless of whether it is paid in a lump or spread out over many years, so long as the present value is held constant. This is the aspect of the theory that leads to the prediction that back-loaded and front-loaded IRAs are equivalent, a prediction that only an economist would make. Suppose it were true. This would imply that firms could attract as many new employees with a retirement bonus as a sign-up bonus, so long as they had the same present value. Automobile manufacturers could sell as many cars with a rebate paid after five years as with one paid at the time of purchase. Both common sense and empirical research suggest that this prediction is also false.

If we want to devise a good saving policy, asking economic theorists is not going to be much help. To whom then can we turn for advice? I recommend four groups of people that might offer helpful advice: dead economists, empirical economists, psychologists, and mothers, not necessarily in that order.

Other Sources of Advice

Economists of prior generations seemed to know much more about how people really behave, and their treatments of saving are particularly illuminating. I have in mind Eugen von Böhm-Bawerk, John Maynard Keynes, and particularly Irving Fisher. Fisher identified three important determinants of saving that are usually omitted by economists: foresight, self-control, and habits. To save, an individual has to have the foresight to recognize a future need, and the self-control to delay gratification. Proper habits can make the self-control easier. Ignoring these factors can lead modern economic theorists astray.

If we are to understand better how self-control and delay of gratification work, some relevant research by psychologists deserves more attention by economists. The distinguished psychologist William James, for example, made the important point that exercising self-control requires effort. In economists' language this means that self-control is costly. The other key point is that temptation matters, a fact most mature adults appreciate.[1] In light of the costs of exerting self-control and facing temptation, most people adopt rules of thumb and engage the help of outside agents to control their behavior. Some of the actions people take seem irrational and bizarre to economists. A well-known example is Christmas clubs, now unfashionable but once a popular institution. Members of a Christmas club would agree to deposit a certain amount in a special account every week for a year. The money in the account earned little or no interest, and the money could not be withdrawn until the following Christmas shopping season. Thus, this financial instrument offered no liquidity, high transaction costs, and a low return. Despite these features, people used the accounts because they wanted to have money to spend for presents and viewed the Christmas club as a good vehicle for accomplishing that end.

To get a sense of the importance of self-control in determining personal saving in this country, it is useful to see just how people save for retirement. Except for the wealthy, most households reach retirement with only three important sources of wealth: social security, private pensions, and home equity.[2] Social security and pensions are psychologically easy ways to save—they require no willpower. Home equity is

145

almost as costless; once the initial down payment is made, paying off the mortgage becomes automatic.[3] The hard ways to save, through liquid assets including stocks and bonds, produce a relatively insignificant contribution toward retirement wealth.

This leads to the obvious conclusion that if we want to encourage family saving, we should do things that facilitate the self-control necessary to delay consumption. This brings us to Mom. It is worth thinking about how a mother would encourage her child to save. A smart Mom is likely to adopt a policy with two features: provide immediate rewards for saving, and put the money where the kid cannot get at it, that is, piggy banks. The old IRA program looks good from this perspective. Taxpayers were given an immediate reward for contributing to an IRA (a reduction in their tax bill), and the money was relatively difficult to withdraw (a penalty for early withdrawal imposed both economic and psychic costs).

The Behavioral Life-Cycle Hypothesis

Just paying attention to this motherly advice would go a long way to improving the analysis of saving policies, but it is possible to go further. Hersh Shefrin and I have formulated a model of saving behavior that incorporates the role of temptation and self-control.[4] Our model departs from the standard life-cycle hypothesis primarily by dropping the assumption of fungibility, implicit in all wealth-based theories of saving. Fungibility is the assumption that money has no labels. A thousand dollars in the checking account is equivalent in every way to the same sum in cash, in stocks, or in home equity (abstracting from liquidity considerations). While satisfying the fungibility assumption is required by economic rationality, in practice most households violate fungibility in important, systematic ways. The violations of fungibility are captured simply by describing the household's system of mental accounts. These mental accounts are the implicit accounting rules households adopt in running their personal finances.

Households vary in the mental accounting procedures that they adopt, but the following stylized description captures much of the flavor of a typical mental accounting system. Suppose a household divides its wealth into four basic mental accounts: current income, liquid assets, home equity, and future income. The current income account is roughly equivalent to a checking account, the liquid assets account is roughly equivalent to a savings account, home equity captures all of housing wealth, and future income includes the present value of future earnings plus the value of pension and social security wealth. According to the life-cycle hypothesis, these four accounts are collapsed into a single number, wealth, which is then allocated evenly across time. In other words, the marginal propensity to consume out of each mental account is assumed to be the same. In the behavioral modification of the life-cycle theory, each mental account has its own marginal propensity to consume. The marginal propensity to consume is close to one from the current income account, positive but much less than one from the liquid asset account, and virtually zero from the home equity and future income accounts. This ordering of marginal propensities to consume follows the level of temptation associated with a positive balance in each account. Households need to exert willpower to resist spending their regular paycheck but find it easy to avoid spending the value of their home or income they will not see until many years later.

Evidence on Mental Accounting

What is the evidence that people distinguish among these accounts? Here the research done by empirical economists comes in handy. My reading of the evidence, drawing on many studies using various data sets from several different countries, is that the mental accounting formulation is strongly supported. Here I will just summarize some highlights.

An important question that has received considerable attention is the effect of pensions on saving. Consider the following experiment. A firm has been offering a defined contribution pension plan in which the firm contributes 5 percent of each worker's income into the plan. The firm then decides to raise the contribution level to 6 percent. What will happen to the workers' savings? Roughly speaking, the life-cycle prediction is that other savings will fall 1 percent; that is, there will be a complete offset. The logic is that if the workers were saving the optimal amount before, they will now substitute the added pension saving for other saving, thus reducing their discretionary saving 1 percent. In contrast, again speaking roughly, the behavioral life-cycle hypothesis predicts no change in other saving, a zero offset. This follows from the assumption that the marginal propensity to consume future income is close to zero, and pension wealth is in the future income mental account. Notice that these rough predictions are very different—a 100 percent offset versus a 0 percent offset.

The empirical estimates on this issue are unequivocal. Most of the estimates of the offset are close to zero; indeed, many of the estimates are actually negative, meaning that when pension wealth increases,

147

other savings also increases. No estimate is remotely close to one.[5]

The same type of result is obtained in examining the effect of housing wealth on other saving. Consider two identical families, with identical life-cycle income streams. One family buys a home, the other rents. When they reach retirement, the home-owning family has $200,000 in home equity. The life-cycle theory predicts that the renting family should save $200,000 more than the home-owning family so that their total assets are equal. Again, this means a complete offset—other saving increases to compensate for the absence of housing wealth. And again, the empirical evidence does not support this prediction. If anything, homeowners save more in other ways than renters, holding everything else including income constant.

The results on pensions and home equity support the view that the marginal propensity to consume from these sources of wealth is close to zero. What about sources of income, especially windfall gains? Here the evidence suggests that the marginal propensity to consume a windfall declines sharply with the size of the windfall. Small windfalls are spent (in fact, the marginal propensity to consume small windfalls is probably greater than one), while large windfalls are at least partly saved. This result is predicted by the mental accounting formulation because large windfalls are more likely to be coded as entering the liquid asset account rather than the current income account. (If you win $50 in the office football pool, you put the money in your pocket; if you win $10,000 in the state lottery, you put the money in your savings account.)

Even the name given to a source of income can affect the way it is allocated. This is illustrated by the case of lump-sum bonuses, such as those common in Japan. Even though these bonuses are quite predicatable, the evidence is that the marginal propensity to consume bonus income is considerably lower than the propensity to consume regular income.[6]

Applications to IRAs

Mental accounting and self-control can provide some insights into the debate about IRAs. I would like to offer four points on this topic.

First, many economists have argued IRAs could not have increased savings because the IRAs would just substitute for other saving. This is our old friend the fungibility assumption, which, I stress, is just an assumption, not a fact. While a rational life-cycle saver would be unaffected by IRAs, real people found them appealing for the reasons cited above: there was an immediate reward for enrolling, and the money was then kept out of sight. Did IRAs simply substitute for other saving? I find the evidence presented by Steven Venti and David Wise quite compelling that IRAs represented primarily new saving. The fact that non-IRA balances remained constant or grew for IRA contributors seems inconsistent with the claim that IRA saving was merely asset shifting.

Second, there is an often-expressed worry that IRA contributors borrowed money to make their contribution. This is a red herring. While on the face of it, such behavior seems to suggest no net saving, this is a short-term perspective. An individual who borrows $2,000 on a credit card to make an IRA contribution will likely pay off the credit card bill well before withdrawing the funds from the IRA account, thereby turning the entire contribution into net saving.

Third, back-loaded IRAs are a bad idea. Regardless of the theoretical equivalence of back-loaded and front-loaded IRAs, undoubtedly back-loaded plans will be much less attractive. If we want to encourage saving, we need to offer immediate inducements. Ironically, the government is trying to get individuals to take a long-term perspective and to save for retirement, while at the same time proposing a plan conceived only to deal with the Congress's short-term concerns with the budget. Congress seems to behave as if cutting taxes now is impossibly costly (either in terms of cutting programs or raising other taxes) while cutting taxes in the indefinite future is free. Perhaps Congress should also be getting some advice from Mom.

Fourth, making IRAs more liquid (by increasing the situations in which money can be withdrawn without penalty) may also be a bad idea. To many savers, a primary attraction of the IRA is precisely its illiquidity. A Christmas club would not work if members could withdraw their money to finance their summer vacation.

Alternative Ways to Increase Saving

I would like to make a few suggestions for other proposals the government could consider as methods of increasing the saving rate. These proposals may strike most economists as odd, but I think Mom would approve.

- Encourage firms to make lump-sum bonuses part of their compensation package. The workers will be happier and will save more.[7]
- Increase withholding rates for the federal income tax, holding the tax rate constant. A large majority of taxpayers already get refunds. Raising the withholding rates will increase this proportion and

increase the average refund. Taxpayers will like the larger refunds, and saving rates will go up.[8]

- Give the middle class a way to apply their refunds to some savings vehicle. Many people failed to contribute to an IRA because they did not have the cash on April 15 and did not want (for mental accounting reasons) to borrow. The refund would be easier to save if it could be done before the check is in hand.

- Encourage firms to offer payroll savings plans. From a mental accounting perspective, the least painful way of parting with money is through a small decrease in the regular paycheck. What you do not see, you do not spend.

- Take actions to facilitate the purchase of a new home. Paying off the mortgage is another easy way to save.

In sum: design savings policies for real people—and listen to Mom.

Notes

Chapter 6: The Effects of Public Policy on Private Saving

1. For a discussion of this problem, see John Helliwell, "The Fiscal Deficit and the External Deficit: Siblings, but Not Twins," in *The Great Fiscal Experiment*, Rudolph G. Penner, ed. (Washington, D.C.: The Urban Institute Press, 1990), pp. 21–58.

2. Robert J. Barro, *The Impact of Social Security on Private Saving: With a Reply by Martin Feldstein* (Washington, D.C.: AEI Press, 1978).

3. For a detailed discussion, see Carolyn L. Weaver, "Support of the Elderly Before the Great Depression," *Cato Journal*, vol. 7 (Fall 1987), pp. 503–25.

4. Related issues are discussed in *Social Security and National Saving*, Rudolph G. Penner, Committee for Economic Development (Washington, D.C.: 1989).

Chapter 7: Past Experience and Current Proposals for IRAs

1. The additional 10 percent tax was a modification of the earlier 10 percent penalty tax levied on withdrawals by the self-employed before age fifty-nine and a half.

2. See Steven F. Venti and David A. Wise, "Tax-Deferred Accounts, Constrained Choices and Estimation of Individual Saving," *Review of Economic Studies*, vol. 52, 1986, pp. 579–601, and William Gale and John Karl Scholz, "IRAs and Household Saving" (July 16, 1990, mimeographed). See also Jonathan Skinner, "Do IRAs Promote Saving? A Review of the Evidence" (March 1991, mimeographed), and Jonathan Skinner and Daniel Feenberg, "Sources of IRA Saving" in Lawrence Summers, ed., *Tax Policy and the Economy* (Cambridge: MIT Press, 1989).

3. Unless otherwise indicated, figures on taxpayer use of IRAs are taken from tabulations of the statistics of income panel of tax returns made available through the University of Michigan.

4. Gale and Scholz, "IRAs and Household Saving," table 1.

5. Seventeen percent of full-time workers had IRAs and 12 percent had IRAs and employer pensions in 1983, as reported by Larry Ozanne and David Lindeman, *Tax Policy for Pensions and Other Retirement Saving* (Washington, D.C.: Congressional Budget Office, 1987), p. 60.

6. Julie H. Collins and James H. Wyckoff, "Estimates of Tax Deferred Retirement Savings Behavior," *National Tax Journal*, December 1988, pp. 565–66.

7. The incentive to consume more could have been offset if the tax reductions received by persons transferring assets into IRAs were accompanied by tax increases on the same or other taxpayers. Whether the expansion of IRAs was accompanied by offsetting tax increases is unclear. The Economic Recovery Tax Act of 1981, which expanded IRA eligibility, clearly added to the deficit. But it is possible that inclusion of IRAs in the bill did not add to the deficit. If IRAs had not been expanded in the bill, for example, other tax reductions could have been included. It is also possible that, in the absence of IRAs, later reductions in the deficit would have been smaller. Thus while the tax reductions of persons transferring assets into IRAs tended to increase their consumption, the net effect on national saving is unclear because the existence of offsets tending to reduce consumption cannot be ruled out.

8. Furthermore, if the IRA earns a steady 8 percent interest rate, funds can be withdrawn after ten years and do better than in a regular savings account despite the 10 percent penalty.

9. Venti and Wise, "Tax-Deferred Accounts, Constrained Choice and Estimation of Individual Saving," pp. 579–601. This study concludes that had the IRA limit been higher in 1982 and early 1983, only between 10 percent and 20 percent of the increased contributions to IRAs would come from reductions in other savings.

10. To lessen the doubt that would otherwise accompany this expansion of savings incentives, monitoring could be set up beforehand to try to measure resulting changes in savings.

11. The withdrawal from the front-loaded IRA in table–4 is the same as it is in table–3. This is because the only tax on the front-loaded IRA is the tax on withdrawal, and the tax rate on withdrawals is 28 percent in each case. The withdrawal from the back-loaded IRA in table 7–4 is the same as from the front-loaded IRA when the man retiring is in the 15 percent tax bracket. The equivalence occurs because of the equivalence between front- and back-loaded IRAs when the tax rate on deposits is the same as the tax rate on withdrawals. In this case the tax rate on deposits is 15 percent for the back-loaded IRA, and it is also 15 percent on withdrawals from the front-loaded IRA.

CHAPTER 8: IRAs AND SAVING

1. Steven F. Venti and David A. Wise, "Government Policy and Personal Retirement Saving," in James Poterba, ed., *Tax Policy and the Economy*, sixth edition (MIT Press, forthcoming in 1992).

2. Based on SIPP data.

3. Venti and Wise, "Government Policy and Personal Retirement Saving."

4. The method for identifying groups of "contributor-like" households is explained in more detail in ibid.

5. Data for 1980 through 1988 is presented in ibid.

6. Data for these two years but including stocks and bonds are shown in ibid.

7. Again, comparable data including stocks and bonds reveal the same pattern and are presented in ibid.

8. The calculations and the data set are explained in detail in Steven F. Venti and David A. Wise, "Heterogeneity, Individual Effects, and IRA Saving: Further Evidence from SIPP," mimeo, 1990.

9. Venti and Wise, "Government Policy and Personal Retirement Saving."

10. For an extreme view, see Jane G. Gravelle, "Capital Gains Taxes, IRAs, and Savings," Congressional Research Service, September 1989; and "Do Individual Retirement Accounts Increase Saving?" *Journal of Economic Perspectives*, vol. 5, 1991, pp. 133–49.

11. For more detail, see Venti and Wise, "Government Policy and Personal Retirement Saving."

12. See Steven F. Venti and David A. Wise, "Tax-Deferred Accounts, Constrained Choice and Estimation of Individual Saving," *Review of Economic Studies*, vol. 53, 1986, pp. 579–601; "IRAs and Saving," in Martin Feldstein, ed., *The Effects of Taxation on Capital Accumulation* (Chicago: University of Chicago Press, 1987); "Have IRAs Increased U.S. Saving? Evidence from the Consumer Expenditure Surveys," *Quarterly Journal of Economics*, vol. 105, 1990, pp. 661–98; and "The Saving Effect of Tax-Deferred Retirement Accounts: Evidence from SIPP," in B. Douglas Bernheim and John Shoven, eds., *National Saving and Economic Performance* (Chicago: University of Chicago Press, 1991).

13. See Venti and Wise, "Tax-Deferred Retirement Accounts: Evidence from SIPP."

14. Venti and Wise, "Have IRAs Increased U.S. Saving?"

15. The evidence is reviewed in Hersh M. Shefrin and Richard H. Thaler, "The Behavioral Life-Cycle Hypothesis," *Economic Inquiry*, vol. 26, 1988, pp. 609–43.

16. See Robin L. Lumsdaine and David A. Wise, "Aging and Labor Force Participation: A Review of Trends and Explanations," National Bureau of Economic Research working paper no. 3420, August 1990 (forthcoming in joint JCER-NBER conference volume, University of Chicago Press).

17. See Steven F. Venti and David A. Wise, "The Determinants of IRA Contributions and the Effect of Limit Changes," in Zvi Bodie, John Shoven, and David A. Wise, eds., *Pensions in the U.S. Economy* (Chicago: University of Chicago Press, 1988).

18. See A. Lans Bovenberg, "Tax Policy and National Saving in the U.S.: A Survey," *National Tax Journal*, vol. 42, 1989, pp. 123–38, for example.

19. It is even difficult to demonstrate a convincing relationship between rather wide-ranging individual tax rates and contributions to tax-deferred saving accounts, controlling for income, age, and other tax-filer characteristics. Daniel Feenberg and Jonathan Skinner, in "Sources of IRA Saving," *Tax Policy and the Economy*, vol. 3, 1989, pp. 25–46, conclude that there is a positive relationship between marginal tax rates and IRA contributions, based on U.S. tax returns. James E. Long, in "Marginal Tax Rates and IRA Contributions," *National Tax Journal*, vol. 43, 1990, pp. 143–53, also concludes that the relationship is positive. But David A. Wise, in "The Effects of Policy Change on RRSP Contributions," prepared for the Tax Policy and Legislation Branch of the Canadian Department of Finance, 1984, finds that the conclusion is extremely sensitive to the functional form used in the statistical

analysis. Indeed, using precise marginal tax rates calculated from tax returns, he finds no relationship between individual marginal tax rates and contributions to Registered Retirement Saving Programs in Canada, controlling for income and other tax-filer attributes, and using a specification that fits the data best. The evidence in Venti and Wise, "The Determinants of IRA Contributions and the Effect of Limit Changes," suggests that the marginal tax rate may be associated with whether a household contributes to an IRA but suggests little relationship to the amount of the contribution.

CHAPTER 9: EXAMINING THE EVIDENCE ON IRAs AND HOUSEHOLD SAVING

1. These figures are taken from B. Douglas Bernheim, *The Vanishing Nest Egg: Reflections on Saving in America* (Twentieth Century Fund, 1991).

2. As proposed, FSAs are commonly referred to as back-loaded IRAs. They allow individuals with incomes below $60,000 and married couples with incomes below $120,000 to make nondeductible contributions of up to $2,500 to qualified accounts. Earnings and contributions retained in the FSA for at least seven years are eligible for full tax exemption when withdrawn. The Bentsen-Roth proposal would allow individuals to contribute up to $2,000 to either a front-loaded (traditional) or back-loaded IRA. Back-loaded contributions can be withdrawn, without tax, after five years.

3. These include William D. Andrews and David F. Bradford, "Savings Incentives in a Hybrid Income Tax System," in Henry J. Aaron, Harvey Galper, and Joseph A. Pechman, eds., *Uneasy Compromise: Problems of a Hybrid Income-Consumption Tax* (Washington, D.C.: Brookings Institution, 1988); Leonard Burman, Joseph Cordes, and Larry Ozanne "IRAs and National Saving," *National Tax Journal*, September 1990; Julie H. Collins and James H. Wykoff, "Estimates of Tax-Deferred Retirement Saving Behavior," *National Tax Journal*, 1987, pp. 561–72; Harvey Galper and Charles Byce, "Individual Retirement Accounts: Facts and Issues," *Tax Notes*, June 2, 1986, pp. 917–21; Jane Gravelle, "Do Individual Retirement Accounts Increase Saving?" *Journal of Economic Perspectives*, Spring 1991, pp. 133–49; R. Glenn Hubbard, "Do IRAs and KEOGHS Increase Saving?" *National Tax Journal*, vol. 37, 1984, pp. 43–54; James A. Long, "Marginal Tax Rates and IRA Contributions," *National Tax Journal*, vol. 43, no. 2 (1990), pp. 143–54; Cherie O'Neil and G. Rodney Thompson, "Participation in Individual Retirement Accounts: An Empirical Investigation," *National Tax Journal*, vol. 47, 1987, pp. 617–24; and Lawrence H. Summers, "Summers Replies to Galper and Byce on IRAs," *Tax Notes*, June 9, 1986, pp. 1014–16.

4. Daniel R. Feenberg and Jonathan Skinner, "Sources of IRA Saving," in Lawrence Summers, ed., *Tax Policy and the Economy* (Cambridge: MIT Press, 1989), pp. 25–46; William G. Gale and John Karl Scholz, "IRAs and Household Saving" (University of California, Los Angeles, and University of Wisconsin–Madison, November 1991, unpublished manuscript); Douglas H. Joines and James G. Manegold, "IRA and Saving: Evidence from a Panel of Taxpayers" (University of Southern California, September 1991, unpublished manuscript); Steven F. Venti

and David A. Wise, "Tax-Deferred Accounts, Constrained Choice and Estimation of Individual Saving," *Review of Economic Studies*, vol. 53, 1986, pp. 579–601; Steven F. Venti and David A. Wise, "IRAs and Saving," in Martin Feldstein, ed., *The Effects of Taxation on Capital Accumulation* (Chicago: University of Chicago Press and NBER, 1987), pp. 7–48; Steven F. Venti and David A. Wise, "The Determinants of IRA Contributions and the Effects of Limit Changes," in Zvi Bodie, John B. Shoven, and David A. Wise, eds., *Pensions in the U.S. Economy* (Chicago: University of Chicago Press and NBER, 1988), pp. 9–52; Steven F. Venti and David A. Wise, "Have IRAs Increased U.S. Saving? Evidence from Consumer Expenditure Surveys," *Quarterly Journal of Economics*, vol. 105, August 1990, pp. 661–98; and Steven F. Venti and David A. Wise, "The Saving Effect of Tax-Deferred Retirement Accounts: Evidence from SIPP," in B. Douglas Bernheim and John B. Shoven, eds., *National Saving and Economic Performance* (Chicago: University of Chicago Press and NBER, 1991), pp. 103–28.

5. Gale and Scholz, "IRAs and Household Saving."

6. Ibid., p. 9. See Robert B. Avery and Gregory E. Elliehausen, "1983 Survey of Consumer Finances: Technical Manual and Codebook" (Board of Governors of the Federal Reserve System, August 1988, unpublished manuscript); and Robert B. Avery and Arthur B. Kennickell, "1986 Survey of Consumer Finances: Technical Manual and Codebook" (Board of Governors of the Federal Reserve System, November 1988, unpublished manuscript), for details about the 1983 and 1986 Survey of Consumer Finance.

7. Martin Feldstein and Daniel R. Feenberg, "Alternative Tax Rules and Personal Saving Incentives: Microeconomic Data and Behavioral Simulations," in Martin Feldstein, ed., *Behavioral Simulation Methods in Tax Policy Analysis* (Chicago: University of Chicago Press and NBER, 1983).

8. Gale and Scholz, "IRAs and Household Saving," table 1.

9. Ibid., table 2.

10. Feenberg and Skinner, "Sources of IRA Saving."

11. Steven F. Venti and David A. Wise, "Government Policy and Personal Retirement Saving" (Dartmouth College and Kennedy School of Government at Harvard, 1991, unpublished manuscript).

12. Chris Carroll and Lawrence H. Summers, "Why Have Private Savings Rates in the United States and Canada Diverged?" *Journal of Monetary Economics*, vol. 20, 1987, pp. 249–79.

13. Jonathan Skinner and Daniel Feenberg, "The Impact of the 1986 Tax Reform on Personal Saving," in Joel Slemrod, ed., *Do Taxes Matter? The Impact of the Tax Reform Act of 1986* (Cambridge: MIT Press, 1990).

14. Ibid., p. 52.

15. See, for example, Laurence J. Kotlikoff, "The Crisis in U.S. Saving and Proposals to Address the Crisis," *National Tax Journal*, vol. 43, no. 3 (1990), pp. 233–46.

16. Gale and Scholz, "IRAs and Household Saving."

17. Treating IRAs as tax deductible is appropriate because our data cover the period, 1983–1985, when all households were eligible for deductible contributions.

18. We limit our sample by eliminating households that either save or dissave

very large amounts. Extensive sensitivity analysis and a discussion of the robustness of our results is presented in Gale and Scholz, "IRAs and Household Saving."

19. Earlier versions of our empirical work contained several ad hoc identification restrictions. As we discuss in the most recent draft of our work, these are not necessary to identify the parameters of the model.

20. Feenberg and Skinner, "Sources of IRA Saving."

21. Feenberg and Skinner, in "Sources of IRA Saving," were the first to mention this in the literature.

22. Richard Thaler, "Anomalies: Saving, Fungibility, and Mental Accounts," *Journal of Economic Perspectives*, Winter 1990, pp. 193–205.

23. See, for example, Hersh M. Shefrin and Meir Statman, "Explaining Investor Preference for Cash Dividends," *Journal of Financial Economics*, vol. 13, 1984, pp. 253–82, for a self-control explanation for the dividend puzzle, and Richard Thaler and Hersh Shefrin, "An Economic Theory of Self-Control," *Journal of Political Economy*, vol. 89, 1989, pp. 392–410, for a number of other interesting examples.

CHAPTER 10: THE ELUSIVE LINK BETWEEN IRAS AND SAVING

1. Steven F. Venti and David Wise, "Tax-Deferred Accounts, Constrained Choice, and Estimation of Individual Saving," *Review of Economic Studies*, vol. 53, 1986, pp. 579–601; Venti and Wise, "IRAs and Saving," in M. Feldstein, ed., *The Effect of Taxation on Capital Accumulation* (Chicago: University of Chicago Press and NBER, 1987), pp. 7–48; Venti and Wise, "Have IRAs Increased U.S. Saving? Evidence from Consumer Expenditure Surveys," *Quarterly Journal of Economics*, vol. 105, 1990, pp. 661–98; William Gale, and John Karl Scholz, "IRAs and Household Saving" (University of California, Los Angeles, 1990, mimeographed).

2. For a more technical discussion of these issues, see Leonard Burman, Joseph Cordes, and Larry Ozanne, "IRAs and National Saving," *National Tax Journal*, vol. 43, September 1990, pp. 259–84; Jane Gravelle, "Do Individual Retirement Accounts Increase Saving," *Journal of Economic Perspectives*, vol. 5, Spring 1991, pp. 133–48; and Jonathan Skinner, "Individual Retirement Accounts: A Review of the Evidence," *Tax Notes*, January 13, 1992.

3. It is true that many families have little liquid saving. Gale and Scholz, for example, calculate that median financial holdings for families who did not purchase IRAs were only $1,500. Median financial wealth is considerably higher among the prime-age savers who are nearing retirement. Median family income among those nearing retirement is $6,600 according to Steven F. Venti and David Wise, "Aging and the Income Value of Housing Wealth," *Journal of Public Economics*, vol. 44, 1991, pp. 371–95.

4. Dieters who previously consumed less than one pint might be induced to increase their ice cream intake.

5. Their simulations are based on small changes in the contribution limit. At this margin, they find little effect, although strictly speaking, one cannot rule out the possibility that inframarginal changes in the IRA program would have had different effects.

6. One could, for example interpret the age-squared term not as an exclusion restriction but as a difference in functional form. The IRA saving equation is linear; the non-IRA saving equation, quadratic.

7. Daniel Feenberg and Jonathan Skinner, "Sources of IRA Saving," in Lawrence Summers, ed., *Tax Policy and the Economy*, vol. 3 (Cambridge, Mass.: MIT Press, 1989), pp. 25–46.

8. Not surprisingly, these families also tend to be wealthier, or earn higher incomes, than the rest of the population.

9. U.S., Internal Revenue Service, *Statistics of Income 1983* (Washington, D.C.: Statistics of Income Division, IRS, 1985), p. 21.

10. Feenberg and Skinner, "Sources of IRA Saving."

11. See Richard Thaler's discussion, chapter 18 in this volume.

CHAPTER 11: IS IT TIME TO ABANDON TAX REFORM?

1. Joel B. Slemrod, ed., *Do Taxes Matter? The Impact of the Tax Reform Act of 1986* (Cambridge, Mass.: MIT Press, 1990).

CHAPTER 12: IRAS, SAVING, AND THE GENERATIONAL EFFECTS OF FISCAL POLICY

1. Alan J. Auerbach, Jagadeesh Gokhale, and Laurence J. Kotlikoff, "Generational Accounts—A Meaningful Alternative to Deficit Accounting," in *Tax Policy and the Economy*, David Bradford, ed., National Bureau for Economic Research, vol. 5 (Cambridge, Mass.: MIT Press, 1991).

2. Steven F. Venti and David A. Wise, "Have IRAs Increased U.S. Savings? Evidence from Consumer Expenditure Surveys," National Bureau of Economic Research working paper no. 2217, April 1987; and Steven F. Venti and David A. Wise, "The Saving Effect of Tax-deferred Retirement Accounts: Evidence from SIPP," mimeo, March 1989.

3. Alan J. Auerbach and Laurence J. Kotlikoff, *Dynamic Fiscal Policy* (Cambridge, England: Cambridge University Press, 1987).

4. Laurence J. Kotlikoff, "The Crisis in U.S. Saving and Proposals to Address the Crisis," in *National Tax Journal* (August 1990).

CHAPTER 14: SOME MEASUREMENT AND POLICY ISSUES OF NATIONAL SAVING AND INVESTMENT

1. Robert S. Chirinko and Robert Eisner, "Tax Policy and Investment in Major U.S. Macroeconomic Econometric Models," *Journal of Public Economics*, vol. 20 (1983), p. 163.

2. One might have thought that an appropriate theoretical formulation was given by Oscar Lange (1938) in his "Optimal Propensity to Consume" article setting forth a model of Keynes's *General Theory*. There is a rate of consumption, private

and public, that will maximize investment. On the one hand, increased consumption will raise the demand for capital to facilitate greater output. On the other, it will reduce investment by raising interest rates (or the supply price of capital goods, thus reducing the marginal efficiency of investment). If consumption is initially at or below this maximization point, reductions in consumption are likely to lower investment, not increase it.

3. Tables with regression results and a fuller discussion are to be found in Robert Eisner, "U.S. National Saving and Budget Deficits," in Gerald Epstein and Herbert Gintis, eds., *The Political Economy of Investment, Saving and Finance: A Global Perspective*, a project of the World Institute for Development Economic Research, United Nations University (Helsinki: forthcoming).

CHAPTER 16: FISCAL POLICY AND THE ECONOMY

1. J. Bradford De Long and Lawrence H. Summers, "Equipment Investment and Economic Growth," National Bureau of Economic Research working paper no. 3515 (November 1990); and J. Bradford De Long, "Machinery Accumulation and Productivity Growth in the Very Long Run: A Five-Nation Look," Harvard Institute of Economic Research, discussion paper no. 1551 (Cambridge, May 1991).

2. Congressional Budget Office, "The Economic Effects of Uncompensated Changes in the Funding of Social Security" (Washington, D.C., April 12, 1991). This number is an average derived from the results of simulations on three growth models.

3. Food Research and Action Center, *Community Childhood Hunger Identification Project, A Survey of Childhood Hunger in the United States: Executive Summary* (Washington, D.C.: FRAC 1991).

CHAPTER 18: HOW TO GET REAL PEOPLE TO SAVE

1. A few economists have recognized the importance of these factors as well, most notably Thomas Schelling, for example, "Self Command in Practice, in Policy and in a Theory of Rational Choice," *American Economic Review*, May 1984, pp. 1–11. For an introduction into the relevant psychological literature, see George Ainslie, "Specious Reward: A Behavioral Theory of Impulsiveness and Impulse Control," *Psychological Bulletin*, July 1975, pp. 463–96: Walter Mischel, "Metacognition and the Rules of Delay," in *Social Cognitive Development: Frontiers and Possible Futures*, eds., J. H. Flavell and L. Ross (New York: Cambridge University Press, 1981); and George Loewenstein and Jan Elster, eds., *Choice over Time* (New York: Russell Sage Foundation, forthcoming).

2. See figure 7–1 in this volume for documentation of this fact.

3. The advent of home equity loans makes spending out of home equity somewhat easier now than it used to be, but refraining from spending out of housing wealth is still easier than refraining from spending this week's paycheck.

4. See Hersh M. Shefrin and Richard H. Thaler, "The Behavioral Life-Cycle

Hypothesis," *Economic Inquiry,* vol. 26, October 1988, pp. 609–43; and Richard H. Thaler, "Anomalies: Savings, Fungibility, and Mental Accounts," *Journal of Economic Perspectives,* Winter 1990. This chapter is based heavily on these two articles.

5. Some authors have argued that this result might be explained by a selectivity bias—workers with a taste for saving go to work for firms with pension plans. No evidence, however, suggests that this explanation is true, and its plausibility is weakened by the fact that even for a sample of workers, all of whom have pension plans, the estimated offset is still negative (wrong sign).

6. See Tsuneo Ishikawa and Kazuo Ueda, "The Bonus Payment System and Japanese Personal Savings," in M. Aoki, ed., *The Economic Analysis of the Japanese Firm* (Amsterdam: North-Holland, 1984).

7. See Daniel Kahneman and Richard H. Thaler, "Economic Analysis and the Psychology of Utility: Applications to Compensation Policy," *American Economic Review,* vol. 81, May 1991, pp. 341–46.

8. Illustrating my profound influence on public policy, the administration has recently moved in exactly the opposite direction suggested here by decreasing withholding rates. Obviously, I think this change was unfortunate.